D1266790

CHRISTIANITY AND THE AFFLUENT SOCIETY

Reginald H. Fuller has also written:
INTERPRETING THE MIRACLES
LUKE'S WITNESS TO JESUS CHRIST
MISSION AND ACHIEVEMENT OF JESUS
NEW TESTAMENT IN CURRENT STUDY
THE FOUNDATIONS OF NEW TESTAMENT CHRISTOLOGY
WHAT IS LITURGICAL PREACHING?

Brian K. Rice has also written:
STEWARDSHIP AND EVANGELISM
WHAT IS CHRISTIAN GIVING?

CHRISTIANITY AND THE AFFLUENT SOCIETY

BY

REGINALD H. FULLER

Baldwin Professor of Sacred Literature
(New Testament) at Union Theological
Seminary, New York City.

AND

BRIAN K. RICE

Education Secretary
United Society for the Propagation
of the Gospel

WM. B. EERDMANS PUBLISHING COMPANY
GRAND RAPIDS   MICHIGAN

PHOTOLITHOPRINTED BY GRAND RAPIDS BOOK MANUFACTURERS, INC.
GRAND RAPIDS, MICHIGAN, UNITED STATES OF AMERICA

1967

PREFACE

WE live in a strange world—so much progress, so many problems; so much prosperity, so many poor. And most of us are so caught up with our prosperity and our problems that we have little time or inclination to reflect on the world around us, let alone evaluate meaningfully the signs of the times. What are we to make of the world in the nineteen-sixties?

We invite you to think with us about Christian responsibility in an affluent society. We have deliberately made this a Transatlantic discussion because the benefits of prosperity and the problems of progress are so evident today in both Britain and America. If one of the results of this investigation is a modest contribution towards Anglo-American understanding and interdependence, this discussion and exchange of views will have been very worthwhile.

Affluence is a good thing: but it is a mixed blessing. Progress has not eliminated hardship or poverty—in many ways these are increasing—and there are urgent problems both in the Welfare State and in the Great Society. We look at some of these vexing problems in detail. Many of them are of world-wide concern and even where this is not so, it is usually the case that America and Britain are grappling with the same basic issues.

Of necessity we are looking at two worlds—the world of the Bible and that of the twentieth century. We are also looking at the world of our human experience in the light of the kingdom of God. In reality this is all the same world at different stages of growth and progress. The world of the Bible and of 1966 is the same material world and, although times have changed, there are many common features and principles which have continued to affect human relationships over the centuries. Our present enquiry looks first at the people of history to see how they responded to wealth and prosperity in Bible times.

And so this is a book about people—about individuals and about communities—about people who live in a problem world. At heart most human problems are theological: they concern

62867

the way we live and the world we live in. We believe this because people matter more than things and because people are children of God. This discussion has sprung out of a burning desire to relate biblical scholarship to the world of the nineteen-sixties and to look at the affluent society in the context of eternity. We found ourselves forced to get out of the study and into the world; to get out of the congregation and into the community. This is the mission of theology.

Several years of preparation and consultation have gone into the background of this biblical and sociological survey, and our enquiries gradually formulated into sequence: (1) the biblical attitudes to wealth and materialism; (2) a close look at contemporary society; and (3) a substantial critique of the affluent society, its premises, goals and achievements, by use of insights provided by the biblical message.

Thus we begin with an extensive survey of the biblical attitude to wealth and this provides the tools for a critique of the world around us, which forms the second part. From the Bible we derive three main insights which are worthy of all men to be received:

1. affluence is the good gift of the Creator God.

2. affluence in the hands of fallen man is a double-edged blessing.

3. Christ has redeemed man, so that in his hands affluence may be used sacramentally as a means of expressing Christian love, both to God and man.

CONTENTS

Acknowledgements

Unless otherwise indicated, passages from the Old Testament quoted in this publication are from the *Revised Standard Version of the Bible,* copyrighted 1946 and 1952.

Verses from the New Testament are from the New English Bible, New Testament, reproduced by permission of the Oxford and Cambridge Presses.

Quotations from Reginald H. Fuller's translation of *The Cost of Discipleship* by Dietrich Bonhoeffer are reproduced by permission of the S.C.M. Press Ltd.

PART ONE

WEALTH IN THE BIBLE

BY REGINALD H. FULLER

1

THE OLD TESTAMENT BACKGROUND

IT is always impossible to approach the New Testament without considering first the Old. The New Testament always takes for granted the teaching of the Old, except where it deliberately corrects it. Thus, for example, the New Testament always takes for granted the Old Testament's view of the world and all the things that are in it as the creation of God.

That God is Creator is not just a speculative philosophical theory, as it was for the Greeks. The Greek philosophers sought for the *arché,* the first principle out of which all else emerged—water, fire, etc., and finally in Aristotle God, the unmoved mover. God the Creator was for the Hebrews a confession of faith. Nor was creation merely something that had happened a few thousand years ago—although creation is told in the form of a story —or rather two alternative stories (Gen. 1–2 :4a, 2 :4b–2 :5). It means that Israelite man confesses his faith that he receives the world as a gift from the Creator at each successive moment of his life.

It seems clear, too, that the Hebrew people never *started* with the idea of God as the Creator. They never thought it was obvious that things in this world came to them in each successive moment as a gift from God. To start with they found Him not in nature, not in creation, but in the events in history, beginning with the event of the exodus in which God had brought His people out of Egypt with a mighty hand and a stretched-out arm. It was through the word which Moses preached to Israel that they could discern the exodus not just as an accident, but as the act of God. And then, in that event, they discerned that the God who did this was the God who was at the back of the universe, the God from whom, at every moment, they received the created world as a gift. Thus, having first of all discerned God in history, particularly in the history of the exodus, they went on to discern this same God as the one who was behind nature and the things of nature. In fact, "nature" is not a Hebraic or Old Testament word at all. For "nature" implies that the world exists in itself of its own momentum, whereas at every moment it is dependent upon God for its being.

This means that what we call nature is there to subserve history. History, unlike nature, is where persons act with purpose, it is also the sphere where God Himself acts. Nature is the stage upon which man acts in history, and God—in certain special events—acts upon man. The material things of this world are used as "props", as it were, on the stage of life. They are subservient to the purposes of man and God, purposes which may conform with one another or may thwart one another—that all depends on man.

This biblical view of the created order and of its relation to history has highly important consequences for the biblical attitude to material riches. Since God created all things and saw that they were good, created things can never be regarded as in themselves evil. That would lead to an asceticism which is completely foreign to the Bible. Of course there is asceticism in the Bible, just as there is a place for asceticism in the Christian life. For example, there were the Nazirites, who took a vow never to touch strong drink. This kind of asceticism has for the rest of community a kind of symbolic significance. It does not mean that material things are evil and should be avoided as much as possible. It says rather that material things are in themselves good, because they have been created by God, but that man can misuse them. He does this by forgetting that they are creations of God, and by exalting them to the level of ultimate or absolute values, making them his ultimate concern. When he does this man falls into idolatry, well described by the Apostle Paul in his letter to the Romans:

"They have made fools of themselves, exchanging the splendour of immortal God for an image shaped like mortal man, even for images like birds, beasts and creeping things . . . they have bartered away the true God for a false one, and have offered reverence and worship to created things instead of to the Creator." (Rom. 1:22–25)

Biblical and Christian asceticism is a protest not against the things of this world in themselves, but against the idolising of the things of this world, making them, in Tillich's meaningful phrase, our "ultimate concern". Puritanism, which has been such a force in British and American life, is a complete misunderstanding of this.

Since, too, the Bible subordinates nature to history, and makes the things of this world tools to be used in carrying out personal purposes—whether of our own, or God's—in history, this means that to secure the material blessings can never be the aim and purpose of religion. This is precisely what the old nature religions sought to do, Baal worship, fertility cults and the like. In them religious observances were performed to make sure of the changing seasons, the spring rain, the summer sunshine, the autumn harvest. There may be elements of Baal worship in popular Christian piety, as there were in Old Testament religion, but these are a corruption of true Christianity. As Luther put it in his blunt and pithy way, God didn't mean us to be fatted hogs. Luther was commenting on the Lord's Prayer and be it noted that the prayer for daily bread is deliberately subordinated to the overall purposes of God in history—the hallowing of His name, the doing of His will, the coming of His kingdom.

We conclude, then, that the doctrine of creation has important consequences for an affluent society. It means, first, that affluence is not itself evil, but a gift of God. It means, secondly, that affluence is given—when it is given—not for selfish enjoyment, but precisely to be the tool by means of which man may carry out certain purposes in history.

No book in the Old Testament deals so fully with affluence and its problems as Deuteronomy. Some of the relevant lessons are well known to Church of England congregations because they occur at Morning or Evening Prayer at Harvest Thanksgiving. These and more, similar, lessons from Deuteronomy are used in the daily lessons of the Episcopal Church in the U.S.A. during the weeks preceding Thanksgiving Day (which falls always on the fourth Thursday in November). Incidentally, it is worth calling attention to the difference between Harvest Thanksgiving of the Church of England and the American Thanksgiving Day, for it has an important bearing on our understanding of the Old Testament's attitude to affluence. In England, the Harvest Thanksgiving usually comes towards the end of September or in early October. The exact date is determined by parish custom or convenience, or, in rural areas, sometimes according to the earliness or lateness of the harvest in any particular year. In so far as any determining factor is present, it is the fact of nature—the fact that this is about the time when "all is safely gathered in". In America, Thanksgiving Day seems, to one brought up in the English custom, unseasonably late. By the last week of November the lovely fall weather, so characteristic of North America, is over, and it is cold and grey. The trees are all bare, and the wonderful autumn colours are gone. Why, one wonders, is harvest thanksgiving postponed so long? Even the churches seem bare (yet not cold, for by that time the central heating is in full blast, though even that seems incongruous!). The answer lies in history—maybe a somewhat legendary history, but an expression of historical consciousness all the same. For the late date of the American Thanksgiving Day originates in the first thanksgiving festival held by the pilgrim settlers (the Pilgrim Fathers who came over one year earlier founded and settled in the Plymouth colony in Massachusetts). This was celebrated as late as December, 1621, owing to the difficult year the colonists had had in sowing and harvesting. So the late date is a reminder of the nation's historical beginnings. It is a thanksgiving for the historical gift of "this good land". It is a recognition that the blessings of nature, the affluence we enjoy, is dependent not only upon nature, but primarily on history. This is what makes the Deuteronomy passages so much more meaningful over here than they are back home in the Old Country :

"For the Lord your God is bringing you into a good land, a land of brooks of water, of fountains and springs, flowing forth in valleys and hills, a land of wheat and barley, of vines and fig trees and pomegranates, a land of olive trees and honey, a land in which you will eat bread without scarcity, in which you will lack nothing, a land whose stones are iron and out of whose hills you can dig copper. And you shall eat and be full, and you shall bless the Lord your God for the good land he has given you." (Deut. 8 : 7–10)
And again :

"When you come into the land which the Lord your God gives you for an inheritance, and have taken possession of it, and live in it, you shall take some of the first of all the fruit of the ground, which you harvest from your land that the Lord your God gives you, and you shall put it in a basket, and you shall go to the place which the Lord your God will choose, to make his name dwell there. . . . Then shall the priest take the basket from your hand, and set it down before the altar of the Lord your God.

"And you shall make response before the Lord your God, 'A wandering Aramean was my father; and he went down into Egypt and so sojourned there, few in number; and there he became a great nation, mighty and populous. And the Egyptians treated us harshly and afflicted us, and laid upon us hard bondage. Then we cried to the Lord, the God of our fathers, and the Lord heard our voice, and saw our affliction, our toil, and our oppression; and the Lord brought us out of Egypt with a mighty hand and an outstretched arm, with great terror, with signs and wonders; and he brought us into this place and gave us this land, a land flowing with milk and honey . . .' " (Deut. 26 : 1–9)

Notice how the Old Testament is quite unashamed of affluence. These passages delight in reciting all the wealth, both vegetable and mineral, which comes from the land. But notice, too, how these things are not just the gifts of nature. They are gifts of God that come from history—from the historical events by which God brought forth His people out of Egypt, into the promised land. So, too, the American Thanksgiving Day is more than a thanksgiving for affluence. It is indeed an affluence at which one can never cease to wonder, when one thinks of the short time in which all this has been achieved—these words are being written on a spot which until 110 years ago was swamp and prairie, where only Indians used to roam. It is a thanksgiving also for history—for an historical deliverance from the bondage of pre-democratic Europe into the land of liberty and opportunity. So perhaps, over here, it is possible more than in Europe to set nature in its proper context of history.

But if history has brought first freedom, and secondly

affluence (and these gifts, if so consciously historical in the United States, are equally the gifts of history in Britain, though perhaps not datably so, at any rate in the national consciousness), freedom and affluence imply responsibility. This is an essential part of Israel's understanding of its history in Deuteronomy. Consider for instance the following points:

1. *It involves, first of all, thankfulness to God*

"You shall bless the Lord your God for the good land he has given you." (Deut. 8 : 10)

"You shall take some of the first of all the fruit of the ground . . . and you shall put it in a basket . . . and you shall go to the priest . . . and the priest shall take the basket from your hand, and set it down before the altar of the Lord your God. . . . And you shall make response before the Lord your God. . . . 'And now, behold, now I bring the first of the fruit of the ground, which thou, O Lord, hast given me.' And you shall set it down before the Lord your God, and worship before the Lord your God ; and you shall rejoice in all the good which the Lord your God has given to you." (Deut. 26)

2. *It involves obedience to God's commandments*

"And now, O Israel, give heed to the statutes and the ordinances which I teach you, and do them, that you may live, and go in and take possession of the land which the Lord, the God of your fathers, gives you." (Deut. 4 : 1)

Deut. 5 : 1–21 (The Ten Commandments). A careful study of these commandments and of the rest of the Deuteronomic laws will indicate that they involve a responsible use of the gifts of affluence which God has given in giving the children of Israel the promised land. They are laws for the responsible use of gifts of God which history and nature have given them.

3. *The laws of God involve the right use of wealth for the neighbour*

The gifts of God in nature and history are not given for us to do what we like with. They are to be used responsibly for the neighbour's good :

"If there is among you a poor man, one of your brethren, in any of your towns within your land which the Lord your God gives you, you shall not harden your heart or shut your hand against your poor brother, but you shall open your hand to him, and shall lend him sufficient for his need, whatever it may be." (Deut. 15:7)

4. *Ownership is not absolute, but relative*

This was already implied in the command to sustain one's needy brother. The poor have a claim on the affluent man's possessions. They are not absolutely his own, to do what he likes with. This is because they are a blessing which he has received from the Lord. When a man forgets this he falls into the illusion of absolute ownership:

"Take heed lest you forget the Lord your God, by not keeping his commandments, and his ordinances, and his statutes which I command you this day: lest, when you have eaten and are full, and have built goodly houses and live in them, and when your herds and flocks multiply, and your silver and gold is multiplied, and all that you have is multiplied, then your heart is lifted up, and you forget the Lord your God, who brought you out of the Land of Egypt. . . . Beware lest you say in your heart, 'My power and the might of my hand have gotten me this wealth'. You shall remember the Lord your God, for it is he who gives you power to get wealth." (Deut. 8:11ff.)

This last quotation brings out a further point. Affluence, since it is a gift of God, is not in itself evil. Yet it does constitute a grave temptation to pride and arrogance: a temptation to forget the Lord, and to imagine we are our own creators.

Affluence, then, according to Deuteronomy, is the gift of God, not only in nature but also in history. This means that it must be used responsibly in the tasks of history. Responsible use means, first, acknowledging God as the giver and source of affluence, not only because He is the God of nature, but primarily because He is the God of history, and because history is the arena of His mighty acts, of His purposes. Secondly it means recognition that men are therefore responsible towards God to obey His will. In particular this means recognition that

B

men are therefore responsible towards God to obey His will. In particular this means that the gifts of affluence are not in our absolute ownership. Man's responsibility is to use them in accordance with God's purposes, recognising, for instance, that the poor brother has a claim upon them. They are not our own to do what we like with.

THE PROPHETS

The increasing affluence of Israel (relatively speaking—it was of course nothing like the affluence of our modern industrial and technological society) in the eighth and seventh centuries led to just these dangers: forgetfulness that affluence was a gift of God, and that it was to be used responsibly towards Him and the neighbour. Hence the prophets are found frequently denouncing the wealthy. To be rich becomes almost the same thing as to be wicked.

> "They sell the righteous for silver,
> and the needy for a pair of shoes." (Amos 2 : 6b)

Wealthy women are denounced as "cows of Bashan"

> "who oppress the poor, who crush the needy." (Amos 4 : 1)

The men

> "Trample upon the poor
> and take from him exactions of wheat . . .
> and turn aside the needy in the gate." (Amos 5 : 11)

So Amos reproaches the people for their luxury:

> "They live in winter houses and summer houses, and houses of ivory." (cf. Amos 3 : 15)

They have a high standard of culture:

> "the noise of songs and the melody of harps." (Amos 5 : 23)

They

> "sing idle songs to the sound of the harp,
> and like David invent for themselves instruments of music."
> (Amos 6 : 5)

They

> "drink wine in bowls
> and anoint themselves with the finest oils." (Amos 6 : 6)

No doubt the herdsman of Tekoa is inclined to voice the protest of the simple countryman against wealth as such, to be opposed not only to luxury but to affluence, and even to culture (cf. his denunciation of music). No doubt, too, he does not recognise, as Deuteronomy more clearly recognises, that wealth is a gift of God, and that it can and must be used responsibly. But Amos was concerned with the actual situation in his day. This was not a time to talk about affluence as a gift of God, but to bring home the irresponsible way in which it was being misused. The teaching of Deuteronomy is more balanced and systematic.

That this was not just the countryman's protest against the high-falutin ways of the city is shown by the fact that Isaiah, who was city bred, and moved with ease in the royal court, joins in the same chorus, condemning the abuses of wealth :

"Your silver has become dross,
    your wine mixed with water.
Your princes are rebels
    and companions of thieves.
Everyone loves a bribe
    and runs after gifts.
They do not defend the fatherless,
    and the widow's cause does not come to them."

(Isa. 1 : 22f.)

Or again :

"The Lord enters into judgment
    with the elders and princes of his people :
It is you who have devoured the vineyard,
    the spoil of the poor is in your houses.
What do you mean by crushing my people,
    by grinding the face of the poor?" (Isa. 3 : 14f.)

There is the same denunciation of luxurious women as in Amos :

"the daughters of Zion are haughty
    and walk with outstretched necks,
    glancing wantonly with their eyes,
mincing along as they go,
    tinkling with their feet." (Isa. 3 : 16)

Then, in the ensuing passages, where he threatens them with punishment, we get a further glimpse of their luxurious living:

> "Instead of perfume there will be rottenness
>   and instead of a girdle, a rope;
> and instead of well-set hair, baldness;
>   and instead of a rich robe, a girding of sackcloth;
> instead of beauty, shame." (Isa. 3:24)

As Peake's commentary says, "Like Amos, he [Isaiah] knew that women, through their ceaseless demands on their menfolk for material things, share fully in the sins of the social order". That is the point. It is not that Amos or Isaiah were Puritans, who considered material things evil or wicked. It is that material things were being misused for personal enjoyment, rather than employed for social justice. Here is exposed one of the chief dangers of an affluent society. It breeds the vices of luxury and leads to the ignoring of the claims of the poor neighbour. The trouble, again, is not with affluence in itself, but with the use, or misuse, that men (and women!) make of it.

Riches can be the source of blessings. It wins you friends, whereas people spurn the poor man:

> "The poor is disliked even by his neighbour,
>   but the rich has many friends." (Prov. 14:20)

Riches give you security:

> "A rich man's wealth is his strong city;
>   the poverty of the poor is their ruin." (Prov. 10:15)

They bring you honour:

> "A poor man is honoured for his knowledge,
>   while a rich man is honoured for his wealth."
>   (Ecclus. 10:30)

There are:

> "Rich men furnished with resources,
>   living peaceably in their habitations." (Ecclus 44:6)

But riches are not an unmitigated blessing. Already a cynical note creeps in a passage like the following:

"A rich man does wrong,
    and he even adds reproaches;
a poor man suffers wrong, and he must add apologies."

(Ecclus. 13:3)

Wealth can make a man self-satisfied and blind to his own faults:

"A rich man is wise in his own eyes,
    but a poor man who has understanding will find him
    out." (Prov. 28:11)

Wealth leads to care and anxiety, and the rich man may envy
the carefree life of the man of modest means:

"Sweet is the sleep of a labourer, whether he eats much
or little; but the surfeit of the rich will not let him sleep."

(Eccles. 5:12)

"Wakefulness over wealth wastes away one's flesh,
and anxiety about it removes sleep." (Ecclus. 31:1)

There are other things in life worth having more than riches:

"A good name is to be chosen rather than great riches,
    and favour is better than silver or gold." (Prov. 22:1)
"I accounted wealth as nothing in comparison of her [sc.
wisdom]." (Wisdom 7:8)
"Better off is a poor man who is well
    and strong in constitution
than a rich man who is severely
    afflicted in body." (Ecclus. 30:14)

It is perhaps no wonder that the wise men of Israel came to
the conclusion that the best thing in life was just a modicum of
this world's goods:

"Give me neither poverty nor riches;
    feed me with the food that is needful for me,
lest I be full, and deny thee,
    and say, 'Who is the Lord?'
or lest I be poor, and steal,
    and profane the name of my God." (Prov. 30:8f.)

Affluence and poverty are equally dangerous. They both lead to the idolatry of material things. They both tempt us to make of material things our ultimate concern, instead of treating them as penultimates. So it would be best to avoid either extreme! The Pastoral Epistles share this same prudential outlook: "There is great gain in godliness with contentment . . . but if we have food and clothing, with these we shall be content". (1 Tim. 6:6f., R.S.V.) But such an outlook is characteristic of the less heroic ages of faith. It appeals to a conservative age, concerned to preserve traditions from the past and hand them on inviolate to the next generation. It is not characteristic of the great creative ages of faith. These are much more heroic. Much more inspiring is the confident cry of St. Paul: "I have learned, in whatever state I am, to be content. I know how to be abased, and I know how to abound. . . . I have learned the secret of facing plenty and hunger, abundance and want." (Phil. 4:11f., R.S.V.) But that it is a secret which, it would seem, the Old Testament has never quite penetrated. It could see that affluence was a gift of God, that it called first for thankfulness for that gift and then for responsible use of it—especially towards the neighbour in need. But bitter experience taught the men of the Old Testament that, man being what he is, affluence was a very dangerous thing, tempting him to forget God the giver of it, and to credit himself with its acquisition, and then, instead of using affluence for the neighbour in his need, to misuse the power affluence gave precisely to exploit the neighbour in his weakness. Better therefore to strike a golden mean—neither poverty nor riches. The Pauline secret of detachment eluded them.

2

JESUS AND WEALTH

WE must not expect to find anything like an exhaustive, systematic teaching about wealth in the recorded sayings of Jesus. Although Jesus was known as a rabbi and although He gave teaching, He was more of a prophet than a rabbi. That is to say, He was a man with a message, a message in particular about what God was doing, what God was doing in history. His message was, "The kingdom of God is at hand". Or, to put it in more modern terms, God is breaking through into history in order to establish His sovereign rule. God's final judgment and salvation are being established. To accept Jesus' message is to accept, in advance, that salvation which will be for the elect at the end of history. Jesus' person is inseparably bound up in His message. In fact, we may say that He is the embodiment and channel of the divine act of judgment and salvation. In Him, in His word and work, the kingdom of God is breaking through. To accept His message is to accept Him, to accept Him is to accept God's salvation. To reject Him and His message is to reject the salvation of God.

> "Happy is the man who does not find me a stumbling block." (Matt. 11 : 6)
> "To receive me is to receive the one who sent me."
> (Matt. 10 :40)
> "Everyone who acknowledges me before men,
> The Son of Man will acknowledge before the angels of God ;
> But he who disowns me before men
> will be disowned before the angels of God." (Luke 12 : 8f.)

Hence, too, the call goes out to men, "follow *me*". To follow Jesus is to accept Him as the embodiment of God's act of salvation, as the embodiment of the kingdom of God. This close connection between following Jesus and accepting the offer of God's kingdom, i.e., of His final salvation, is shown by such passages as :

"To another he said, 'Follow me', but the man replied, 'let me go and bury my father first'. Jesus said, 'Leave the dead to bury their dead; you must go and announce the kingdom of God'.

"Yet another said, 'I will follow you, sir; but let me first say good-bye to my people at home'. To him Jesus said, 'No one who sets his hand to the plough and then keeps looking back is fit for the Kingdom of God'." (Luke 9:49ff. par.)

The above quotations introduce another important aspect of the call to follow Jesus. To respond to that call is to make a complete break with the whole of one's past. It involves the surrender of all family ties: "Let the dead bury their dead"—even to go back and say goodbye to one's parents would be a rejection of the call. Here is a typical oriental exaggeration, but it brings out the absolute claim of discipleship. It was just like this with Peter, and Andrew, with James and John:

"Jesus was walking by the shore of the Sea of Galilee when he saw Simon and his brother Andrew on the lake at work with a casting-net; for they were fishermen. Jesus said to them, 'Come with me, and I will make you fishers of men'. And they at once left their nets and followed him.

"When he had gone a little further he saw James son of Zebedee and his brother John, who were in the boat overhauling their nets. He called them and, leaving their father Zebedee in the boat with the hired men, they went off to follow him." (Mark 1:16–20)

It was a breach with all family ties to follow Jesus. These ties had to be broken completely. But not only family ties; also their businesses. So it was too with Levi the publican:

"As he went along, he saw Levi, son of Alphaeus at his seat in the custom-house, and he said to him, 'Follow me'; and Levi rose and followed him." (Mark 2:14)

Later on as Peter looked back at his call, he reminded Jesus how he had left all in order to follow Him: "We here have left everything to become your followers". (Mark 10:28)

Some of Dietrich Bonhoeffer's comments on these scenes, the call of the first disciples, are worth recalling here:

"If we would follow Jesus we must take certain definite steps. The first step, which follows the call, cuts the disciple off from his previous existence. . . . To stay in the old situation makes discipleship impossible. Levi must leave the receipt of custom and Peter his nets in order to follow Jesus. One would have thought that nothing so drastic was necessary at such an early stage. Could not Jesus have initiated the publican into some new religious experience and leave him as he was before? He could have done so had he not been the incarnate Son of God. But since he is Christ, he must make it clear from the start that his word is not an abstract doctrine, but the re-creation of the whole life of man. The only right and proper way is quite literally to follow Jesus. . . .

". . . So long as Levi sits at the receipt of custom, and Peter at his nets, they could both pursue their trade honestly and dutifully, and they might both enjoy religious experiences, old and new. But if they want to believe in God, the only way is to follow his incarnate Son." (D. Bonhoeffer, *The Cost of Discipleship*, 1959, pp. 52f.)

This radical demand to leave all and follow Jesus does not mean that Jesus rejects the Old Testament and its healthy realism which believes that all life is good—family relations and the business of the work-a-day world. But it does mean that in the presence of the revelation of Ultimate Reality all less than ultimate realities such as family and business ties have to be seen for what they are—not ultimate but penultimate realities, and they have to give way before the Ultimate.

Among these less than ultimate realities is the reality of riches, of wealth, of affluence. Here is another story of a would-be follower of Jesus:

"As [Jesus] was starting out on a journey, a stranger ran up, and, kneeling before him, asked, 'Good Master, what must I do to win eternal life?' Jesus said to him '. . . You know the commandments: Do not murder; do not commit adultery; do not steal; do not give false evidence; do not defraud; honour your father and mother'. 'But, Master', he replied, 'I have kept all these since I was a boy.' Jesus looked straight at him; his heart warmed to him, and he said, 'One thing you lack: go sell everything you have and give to the poor . . . and come, follow me'. At these words his face fell and he went away with a heavy heart; for he was a man of great wealth." (Mark 10:17–22)

In this story there is no question of riches being evil—such a view was impossible, given the biblical doctrine of creation. The rich young man is not being advised to complete his ethical perfection by adding to his keeping of the commandments a further commandment, namely the ascetic practice of holy poverty. If he did that he would still be lacking the "one thing" —that is, discipleship to Jesus, acceptance of the kingdom of God, of the presence in Jesus of God's salvation. For him, this meant surrender of all his wealth and giving to the poor as a precondition of discipleship. But in the moment of decision this is precisely what he refused to do. At that moment, he exalted wealth—one of the good, penultimate things of life—to the status of an ultimate. He made wealth his god. Luther comments: " 'One thing': that is, what you lack is everything. For you would be devout, and yet you refuse to give up your goods for my sake, and to suffer with me. Therefore Mammon is your God, and you prefer it to me." There is no suggestion that the young man had not obeyed the first commandment before, that he had previously made Mammon his god. He decides to do so now in the moment of decision, when confronted by the offer of the kingdom or salvation of God present in the person of Jesus. This shows that we cannot extract from this story a generalised ethic. Jesus does not say to all men "Get rid of your wealth: it is an evil, it distracts you from the main task of life". What He does say is to the particular young man in a particular situation —he wants to inherit eternal life: "If that's what you want to do, now you must choose between the old life and the new. You must make a complete breach with your past and come and follow me". Only in the moment of decision does he exalt his wealth to the status of the ultimate and make it his god.

This demand for a radical decision involving a complete breach with the past Jesus drives home with His parables. This is the point of the twin parables of the hid treasure and the pearl of great price:

"The kingdom of Heaven is like treasure in a field. The man who found it buried it again; and for sheer joy went and sold everything he had and bought that field.

"Here is another picture of the kingdom of Heaven. A merchant looking out for fine pearls found one of special value; so he went and sold everything he had, and bought it." (Matt. 13 :44–46)

We could almost imagine Jesus challenging the rich young man in Mark's story with these two parables. Nothing is too precious to surrender for the sake of the Ultimate—God's salvation, present in Jesus.

It is the same requirement of radical decision that Jesus inculcates in His little sayings about drastic self-mutilation—again a typical oriental exaggeration :

"If your hand is your undoing, cut it off; it is better for you to enter life [i.e., into the kingdom of God] maimed than to keep both hands and go to hell and the unquenchable fire. And if it is your foot that leads you astray, cut it off; it is better to enter into life a cripple than to keep both your feet, and be thrown into hell. And if it is your eye, tear it out; it is better to enter into the kingdom of God with one eye than to keep both eyes and be thrown into hell." (Mark 9 :43–47)

Closely connected with the same line of thought is the parable of the great feast :

"Jesus answered, 'A man was giving a big dinner party and had sent out many invitations. At dinner-time he sent his servant with a message for his guests, "Please come, everything is now ready". They began one and all to excuse themselves. The first said, "I have bought a piece of land, and I must go and look over it; please accept my apologies". The second said, "I have bought five yoke of oxen, and I am on my way to try them out; please accept my apologies". The next said, "I have just got married and for that reason I cannot come".' " (Luke 14 : 16–20)

Jesus does not mean to suggest that there is anything wrong in themselves with the pursuit of business interests—buying a piece of land or five yoke of oxen, or with domestic responsibilities, such as getting married. His parables are not general moral teaching, but intended to challenge men in concrete situations. When men are confronted by the challenge "Follow me" nothing must be allowed to stand in the way, not even business or domestic affairs. We cannot use these challenges to elaborate a general ethic of asceticism, as though Jesus were inculcating poverty for its own sake. In certain concrete situations, the call to discipleship, the call to accept God's offer of His kingdom, His salvation, demands precisely the surrender of all earthly concerns. But it is not a universal rule.

Is there then any universal rule? Is there a demand which is placed on all who would follow Jesus—or, to put it in the language of the Church after the resurrection—to become Christians, members of Christ's body? If there be any such universal rule, we may state it in terms of total commitment. Total commitment—that is what is demanded of Christian believers. Total commitment means surrendering to Him not a part, but the whole of our lives. Henceforth all that we have and are belongs to Him.

What does this involve with regard to the things of this world, our domestic responsibilities, the things we possess? Again Dietrich Bonhoeffer has significant insights to offer us here. He says:

"The call of Jesus teaches us that our relation to the world has been built on an illusion. All the time we thought we had enjoyed a direct relation with men and things. . . . Now we learn that in the most intimate relationships of life, in our kinship with father and mother, brothers and sisters, in married love, and in our duty to the community direct relationships are impossible. Since the coming of Christ, his followers have no more immediate realities of their own, not in their family relationships nor in the relationships formed in the process of living. Between father and son, husband and wife, the individual and the nation, stands Christ the mediator. . . . We cannot establish direct contact outside ourselves except through him, through his word, and through our following of him." (D. Bonhoeffer, op. cit., p. 86)

Thus, having taken away our whole lives everything we have and are, our personal ties to family, our wealth, Christ *may* give it back to us again:

"At this Peter spoke, 'We here', he said, 'have left everything to become your followers'. Jesus said, 'I tell you this: there is no one who has given up home, brothers or sisters, mother, father or children, or land, for my sake and for the Gospel, who will not receive in this age a hundred times as much—houses, brothers and sisters, mothers, children and land—and persecutions besides; and in the age to come eternal life'." (Mark 10 :28–30)

Christ, then, may give us back everything we had surrendered to Him. But when it is thus given back, it will not be the same. With typical oriental exaggeration, He says again, we shall get back a hundredfold more. What does this mean? Surely not that becoming a Christian is a sound investment! Rather, it means that all we get back is now given to us as part of the new life in Christ, used, so far as we need it, entirely in the service of the kingdom of God. They no longer become objects of selfish concern. Christ, as it were, doles out to His disciples just as much as they need for the life of discipleship. The disciples are to look to that life, not to earthly possessions :

"Do not store up for yourselves treasure on earth, where it grows rusty and moth-eaten, and thieves break in to steal it. Store up treasure in heaven, where there is no moth and no rust to spoil it, no thieves to break in and steal. For where your wealth is, here will your heart be also." (Matt. 6 : 19–21)

The man who lays up treasures on earth—i.e., who devotes himself to gathering affluence for its own sake, allows things, as Bonhoeffer would put it, to come between Christ and himself. Christ has doled out to His followers, as it were, what they have surrendered to Him, but these things are received back only as a gift from Him, to be used in His service. The hearts of His followers are set upon Him. To set one's heart on something is to be totally committed to it. You cannot be totally committed to Christ and to earthly goods. You cannot serve God and Mammon. You cannot have two absolutes. For the disciple, only Christ is Ultimate Reality. Penultimate realities, earthly goods, when given back to Him, fall into their proper place, precisely as penultimate goods. But the man who treats penultimate realities as though they were ultimates becomes a prey to anxiety :

"Therefore I bid you put away anxious thought about food and drink to keep you alive, and clothes to cover your body. Surely life is more than food, the body more than clothes. Look at the birds of the air; they do not sow and reap and store in barns, yet your heavenly Father feeds them. You are worth more than the birds! Is there a man of you who by anxious thought can add a foot to his height? And why be anxious about clothes? Consider how the lilies grow in the fields; they do not work, they do not spin; and yet, I tell you, even Solomon in all his splendour was not attired like one of these. But if that is how God clothes the grass in the fields, which is there today, and tomorrow is thrown on the stove, will he not all the more clothe you? How little faith you have! No, do not ask anxiously, 'What are we to eat? What are we to drink? What shall we wear?' All these are things for the heathen to run after, not for you, because your heavenly Father knows that you need them all. Set your mind on God's kingdom and his justice before everything else, and all the rest will come to you as well. So do not be anxious about tomorrow; tomorrow will look after itself. Each day has troubles enough of its own." (Matt. 6 : 25–34)

All this is not just a prescription for mental health. The real point lies in the final charge: "Set your mind on God's kingdom and his justice before everything else". The disciple is one completely committed to God and His purpose in the world, and complete commitment means that he has handed over to Christ his whole life, everything he is and has. Henceforth he has a direct relation, as Bonhoeffer put it, only with Christ. Christ *may* give back worldly possessions to him—perhaps nothing, perhaps in part, perhaps *in toto,* as He decides is necessary for the carrying out of God's purposes. But then, whatever we receive back, our relation with them is not a direct one, only indirect, only through Christ, so that we are responsible to Him for whatever use we make of them. He has an absolute claim over them. If however we are anxious about worldly things, then we are trying to re-establish a direct relation with things. Only God has a direct relation to things. So in being anxious for things we are putting ourselves once more in the place of God, listening to the serpent's primal temptation, "You shall be as gods". (Gen. 3 : 5, E.R.V.) That, as Bonhoeffer again has suggested, provides the test as to whether we are using the goods that Christ has given back to us in a legitimate way, or whether we are indulging in unlawful accumulation :

"But where are we to draw the line between legitimate use and unlawful accumulation? Let us reverse the word of Jesus and our question is answered: 'Where thy heart is, there shall thy treasure be also'." (op. cit., p. 156) He goes on to point out that it makes no difference whether our "treasure" is large or small—or, as we have put it, whether when we become disciples and give over all we have and are to Christ and He gives us some of it back, it be a small amount or much. To be "rich" in the things of this world is to set one's heart upon them, to suppose that it is our job instead of God's to secure them and assure our possession of them, in short, to try to do God's work for Him, to put ourselves in the place of God. Thus the rich man may be economically poor. The rich man is the man whose heart is set upon worldly goods, whether they are goods he already has, or goods he longs or hopes to acquire.

Of course, it is so easy to "kid" ourselves that we are seeking God's kingdom and His righteousness, when actually we are being anxious about worldly goods. Thus, once more, Bonhoeffer: "anxiety for food and clothing is clearly not the same thing as anxiety for the kingdom of God, however much we should like to persuade ourselves that when we are working for our families and concerning ourselves with bread and houses we are thereby building the kingdom, as though the kingdom could be realised only through our worldly cares". (op. cit., p. 160) ". . . Worldly cares are not a part of our discipleship, but distinct and subordinate concerns. Before we start taking thought for our life, our food and clothing, our work and families, we must seek the righteousness of Christ." (Ibid.)

No wonder, then, Jesus said, "How hard it will be for the wealthy to enter into the kingdom of God. . . . It is easier for a camel to pass through the eye of a needle than for a rich man to enter the kingdom of God." (Mark 10:23, 25) No wonder the disciples asked, "Then who can be saved?"! (v. 26) For Jesus had defined wealth and poverty not in terms of bank balances, but in terms of where one's heart is. So then, Jesus quite frankly admits: "For men it is impossible, but not for God; to God everything is possible". Humanly speaking it is impossible for any man to become a disciple of Jesus, for it means becoming what he cannot be—one whose heart is set upon God and His righteousness, His kingdom, His purposes, whereas man's heart is set upon his own purposes. But God gives discipleship as a gift, and thereby He transforms the heart of man, so that it is set no longer on the things of this world, but upon God and His righteousness, His kingdom, His purposes. Salvation through following Jesus is solely the gift of God. Salvation means ceasing to be "rich" in the biblical sense of the word; that is, making things, and therefore in the last analysis self, into gods. To dethrone self is a hard thing—but with God all things are possible.

THE POOR

Jesus lived mainly among the poor, and was a poor man Himself: "Foxes have their holes, the birds their roosts; the Son of Man [probably originally Jesus simply said 'I', and in any case was referring to Himself] has nowhere to lay his head". (Matt. 8 : 20 par.)

His sympathies were with the poor. So we learn from the story of the widow's mite, which certainly sounds like a genuine memory about Jesus:

"Once he was standing opposite the temple treasury, watching people as they dropped their money into the chest. Many rich people were giving large sums. Presently there came a poor widow who dropped in two tiny coins, together worth a farthing [American R.S.V. says 'two copper coins which together make a penny: the American penny is about the size of the now obsolete English farthing'.] He called his disciples to him. 'I tell you this', he said, 'this widow has given more than any of the others; for those others who have given had more than enough, but she, with less than enough, has given all she had to live on.' " (Mark 12 : 41–44)

Here is an actual incident at once pressed by Jesus into a parable. It is a challenge to total commitment. The woman gave all that she had: so Jesus demands total commitment for the kingdom of God. It puts the "rich" to shame, and illustrates the saying about the difficulty the rich find in entering into the kingdom of God. It is not just a general piece of teaching, suggesting that there is something more virtuous about poverty than wealth. But it shows the kind of people with whom Jesus, humanly speaking, had a natural sympathy.

At the same time He has no social theory about the redistribution of wealth, no anti-poverty programme, like President Johnson. While He tells the rich young man to sell all he has and give to the poor (as the obvious way of getting rid of his wealth, which was for him a barrier to discipleship) He makes the realistic *obiter dictum* in the story of the anointing at Bethany : "You have the poor among you always, and you can help them whenever you like". (Mark 14 : 7) Jesus was not concerned with a social programme. That would only have applied to a temporary concrete situation. Nor does He lay down any social principle. He simply came to confront men with the challenge of the kingdom of God. Rich men, poor men were confronted with that challenge. Poor men were, He noticed empirically, more ready to hear that message. But there was no virtue in poverty as such, just as wealth in itself was not necessarily an insuperable barrier to accepting his message, since with God all things were possible. Thus "rich" and "poor" are words which in Jesus tend to glide into words denoting a man's relation and attitude to God.

JESUS—MAN OF HIS AGE, OR MAN FOR ALL TIMES ?

Two things seem to stand in the way of taking Jesus' teachings as truths for all times and for all sorts and conditions of men. To begin with, He was a first-century Palestinian Jew, sharing all the limitations of His contemporaries. Such a statement may seem shocking to some who are unfamiliar with the whole trend of modern New Testament scholarship. The devout Christian believer generally starts by assuming that Jesus Christ is God—or at least a kind of demi-God—and that therefore His message and His teachings are, taken as they stand, valid for all time. Even Christian theologians—especially "systematic" theologians, who tend to think in philosophical abstractions rather than to let their thought be guided by the biblical message and by the historical study of the Bible—tend to make the same assumption. It cannot be too strongly asserted that the incarnation—the doctrine that Jesus is true God as well as true man—

c

is a confession of faith which comes *after* we have met Jesus, both in His earthly life, and as risen. We shouldn't start out with belief in the incarnation, and then try to fit Jesus' historical life and teaching into it. It was only after Thomas had met the risen Lord that he could cry "My Lord and my God". (John 20 : 28) So we have to start with Jesus as a man, as a man of the first century, as a Palestinian Jew. If we do, then it occasions no surprise that He does not teach anything which has directly to do with the modern problems of a "world come of age", an enlightened, emancipated society, an age of industrial and technological efficiency and achievement, of nuclear power and automation. Jesus simply took for granted an agricultural society in a backward province of the Roman Empire, where most things were beyond human control because they were controlled either by nature or determined by the occupying power. He did not speak to men who had decisions to make beyond the ordinary personal day-to-day level—a judge being pestered by an importunate widow, a father having to decide whether to take back his wayward son. We can hardly therefore be surprised that there is no teaching on social, political or economic questions which so concern us. He never addressed the decision-makers of His own day, let alone ours.

But there is not only what Jesus shared with His contemporaries. There is also that which was peculiar to Himself. He proclaimed, as we have seen, the breaking in of the kingdom of God : The Reign of God is at hand. He proclaimed that all this present world and all its feverish activity is shortly to come to an end. How then could He be overly concerned with the carrying on of the world and its business? Our answer to this will depend upon our understanding of Jesus' meaning when He preached the nearness of the kingdom of God, which was already breaking through. Did He really believe that the world was shortly to come to an end? Did He not rather use this framework, derived from late Jewish apocalyptic, in order to proclaim the immediacy and finality of the salvation He had come to offer? It is not just that the imminent expectation of the end was disappointed and had to be put off later and later by the Church, but rather that the earliest Church, under the impact of the

resurrection appearances, expressed its overwhelming certainty
of the salvation accomplished by Jesus by proclaiming His
speedy return. Partly they were right—right in their overwhelming certainty. Partly they were wrong, whenever they mistook this
mode of expressing their overwhelming certainty for a chrono-
logical timetable. Then they got into the difficulties, and those
who followed them were obliged to put off the return of Christ,
first to some later date (within this generation, but not immediately, Mark 9 : 1) and finally to the Greek calends—"a thousand years in God's sight are but as a day". (II Peter 3 : 8) For
us it is time to understand aright what Jesus meant by His
proclamation of the imminence of the end, viz. the ultimacy and
finality of the salvation (and judgment) He came to offer, and
what the earliest Church really meant—even it did not fully
understand it—by the imminent return of Christ—namely the
overwhelming certainty of the final and ultimate salvation He
has brought. This final and ultimate salvation which Jesus has
brought, this possibility of realising already here and now what
human life was destined by God to be, confronts us with the
demand and the possibility of fulfilling the demand of the love
of God and neighbour. And the world, in which we are placed,
and in which the Old Testament sees the creation of God Himself—is the arena where this command to love the neighbour is
to be implemented. Rightly understood, the message of Jesus
does not invite us to escape the world and its tasks, as though
the world were shortly coming to an end, but confronts us with
an offer (forgiveness of sins and freedom therefore to love God
and the neighbour) and a demand (to love the God and the
neighbour) in the world and its concrete situations.

Of course, the situation in which the earliest Christians—like
Jesus Himself—found themselves was not a situation where they
were called upon to exercise any responsibility for the ordering
of the world. They were provincial subjects of the Roman
Empire. We at least in Britain and America are responsible members of a democracy. We participate, in one way or another, in
the political, economic and social decisions of our nations. And
so upon us is laid the responsibility—as well as the freedom—
to implement the commandment of love within those respon-

sibilities. Jesus' teaching about riches represents one area in which the commandment of love had a special relevance in His own day. We cannot read off the demand with which He confronted the men and women of His day and age and treat it as though it were immediately transferable to ours. Such a procedure might in fact lead to the precise opposite of love—a mere conservative or reactionary acceptance of the *status quo* justified by the letter of scripture, as for instance when it is claimed that Jesus was only concerned with "spiritual" things, and that therefore clergymen have no right to preach politics from the pulpit or nuns to join picket lines. We have to take His concrete commands as illustrations of what love meant for His day and age, not what it means for ours. We then have to ask ourselves what does the demand of love mean for us in our situation. Mr. Rice's painstaking investigation of the situation which confronts us in the modern world provide the context in which this has to be worked out.

This does not mean that the early Christian belief in the imminent return of Christ has completely lost its relevance today. Far from it. It serves as a constant reminder of the incompleteness of all earthly achievements. It shows that even Christian achievement in obedience to the law of love in concrete situations is always provisional. Christians can never "build the kingdom of God" on earth—such language is completely foreign to the New Testament. There you can *receive* the kingdom of God, *enter* it, *seek* it. There you can *witness* to the kingdom of God, and *suffer* for it. But you can never *build* it or *extend* it or *spread* it. All of these do-it-yourself notions, much as they appeal to the activistic Anglo-Saxon mind, are utterly alien to the New Testament, and it is high time they were purged from Christian vocabulary. Rather, it is the Christian task, by obeying the commandment of love in the concrete situation in which he is placed—which, in our western democracies, involves political, social and economic responsibilities—to shape society into some sort of approximation to the perfect society of the kingdom of God. All historical societies contain within themselves the seeds of their own destruction. Thus even the most "Christian" political, social and economic order is at best a tem-

porary and preliminary reflection of the kingdom of God, which
lies at the end of all history. Such is the relevance of the early
Christian belief in the speedy return of Christ for us today.

Thus while Christian faith in Jesus Christ as the disclosure of
God and His purpose forbids us to take refuge in a complete
other-worldliness and plunges us into this world as the arena of
our obedience, it equally forbids us to take this world too
seriously, because it can never become the kingdom of God until
Christ returns and history comes to an end. Christian faith is
thus our protection against limiting our Christian obedience to
private life or to life within the four walls of the sanctuary. But
at the same time it prevents us from taking economic, social and
political life with ultimate seriousness. The Church proclaims
the future, coming kingdom of God which neverthelesss is already
preliminarily at work in Christian obedience to the commandment of love.

3

THE FIRST CHRISTIAN COMMUNITY

BETWEEN Jesus and the Church there stood a crucial turning-point—the revelation of Jesus as risen from the dead. This meant that the earliest community could no longer go on simply repeating the message of Jesus Himself. It could no longer proclaim that the kingdom of God was at hand, and just beginning to break through in the words and deeds of Jesus. The resurrection appearances revealed to the disciples that with Jesus' mission and achievement the kingdom of God had in fact been decisively inaugurated, though it still awaited final consummation. Consequently there was a radical change in the message of the Church, as compared with the message of Jesus. Whereas Jesus proclaimed the kingdom of God, the Church proclaimed Jesus. This does not mean that the Church got Jesus all wrong. It is the necessary adjustment consequent upon the decisive turning point. Jesus' own message was now in a very real sense out of date, for since then, He had died and had been raised from the dead, with all that that meant for the coming of the kingdom of God.

Jesus had called men and women to accept His message and to follow Him. The early Church calls men and women to repent, which meant quite concretely, for the first hearers, to revise their whole attitude to Jesus after they had participated in His crucifixion, to accept Him and all that He had stood for after they had rejected Him. This repentance corresponds— *mutatis mutandis*—to Jesus' challenge to men to accept His own message. Then, in place of Jesus' call, "Follow me", comes the challenge: "submit to baptism" (see Acts 2:38).

Baptism brought the baptised into an already-existing community, with a distinctive common life of its own. This life is summarised by the author of Acts in the classic words:

"They met constantly to hear the apostles teach and to share the common life, to break bread and to pray." (Acts 2:42)

The important phrase for us to notice here is, "to share the common life". The Greek word for "common life" is *koinonia*—a word not unknown in many Christian circles today. It is sometimes translated "fellowship" and sometimes "communion". None of these translations brings out the full meaning of the word. "Fellowship" too often suggests a hearty, backslapping camaraderie, an artificial friendliness towards people you don't really care about, something which is no more than skin deep, a mere frothy emotion. Even at its best it is something that exists, as it were, purely on the horizontal plane, a relation among men. "Communion" is better, for we often associate that word with our vertical relationship with God. The New Testament for instance speaks of our communion or participation (here is another word for *koinonia*) in the life in Christ, in all the benefits of His salvation. Thus, in I Corinthians 10 : 16, when the Apostle speaks of the Lord's Supper, he uses the word *koinonia* :

"When we bless 'the cup of blessing' is it not a means of sharing (*koinonia*) in the blood of Christ? When we break the bread, is it not a means of sharing in the body of Christ?"

Or again, when he greets the same Corinthians at the conclusion of his severe letter to them (II Cor. 10–13) he writes of *koinonia* in the Holy Spirit :

"The grace of the Lord Jesus Christ, and the love of God, and the fellowship [*koinonia*] in the Holy Spirit, be with you all." (II Cor. 13 : 14)

But just as the word fellowship, used by itself, too readily suggests a purely "horizontal", humanly-contrived togetherness, so too the word communion suggests too much a purely "vertical" relationship to God, Christ and the Holy Spirit. While the word "communion" asserts a vital truth, over against all purely human, this worldly conception of the Christian common life, it fails perhaps to express fully the equally important horizontal dimension which the vertical dimension creates. It is altogether too "spiritual" a word, too confined to our relationship with God. Nor is *koinonia* a purely "spiritual" relation with our fellow men either. It denotes a relationship with our fellow Christians which certainly has its base in the spiritual, in our sharing the blessings of our common salvation, communion in the body and blood of Christ, our oneness in Christ, our participation in His body and blood, our sharing of the Holy Spirit and His gifts. Equally certainly, too, does this common participation lead to a new spiritual relationship with our fellow-believers. But at the same time it creates a relationship which finds its fullest expression in the material sphere. This is brought out two verses later, following the classical description of the life of the earliest Christian community:

"All whose faith had drawn them together held everything in common: they would sell their property and possessions and make a general distribution as the need of each required." (Acts 2:44f.)

This is often referred to as the early Christian "communism". But, as has not infrequently been pointed out, it is really nothing of the kind. Obviously it is not communism in the modern political sense. It is not a political, social and economic ordering of society based on Marxist theory, as in the Communist countries today. It has nothing whatever to do with the production of economic wealth. Indeed, its failure to provide for this has often been seen as the cause of its later supposed breakdown which, it is held, led in turn to the great poverty of the Jerusalem Church and to Paul's collection for them, about which we shall speak in a later chapter. Whatever it was, it was certainly not enforced as a law. Rather, it was a spontaneous expression of *agape* (Christian love) and *koinonia*. And as has frequently been pointed out, the fault of Ananias and Sapphira in Acts chapter 5 was not that they refused to obey the law for the Christian community, but that they put on an act of deception, pretending that they had given up all their goods, when in fact they had kept back a part.

A great deal of confusion has been thrown into the problem of this so-called early Christian communism by the discovery of the Dead Sea Scrolls. There we read in the so-called Manual of Discipline (I QS 1:12):

"And all who have offered themselves for his truth shall bring all their knowledge and strength and wealth into the community of God, to purify their knowledge in the truth of God's

statutes, and to distribute their strength according to the perfection of his ways and all their property according to his
righteous counsel." [1]

Similarly, in the rules for the admission of new members to
the community we read :

"His wealth and his wages shall be put at the disposal of the
man who has supervision over the wages of the masters, and he
shall enter it in the account at his disposal, but shall not spend
it for the masters." (I QS 6 : 19–20) [2]

At first sight it is tempting to suppose that the earliest Christian community simply took over the rule of common life from
the covenanters at Qumran. Actually, however, there is an all
important difference. The community of goods at Qumran was a
rule. You accepted it as part of your obligations as members of
the community. It was, presumably, rigorously enforced. In fact,
we hear that punishment was stipulated for those who lied to
the Qumran community as Ananias and Sapphira lied to the
Church :

"If there is found among them a man who lies about his
wealth, and knows it, he shall be excluded from the sacred food
of the masters for a year, and shall be deprived of a fourth of
his food ration." (I QS 6 : 24f.)

At first sight it looks as though Peter were enforcing the same
rule in the Christian community. But it is to be noted that the
punishment of Ananias and Sapphira was *death*—not just demo-
tion to the novitiate. Can we suppose that Peter was enforcing
an even stricter rule than that which prevailed at Qumran? To
be struck dead is far more severe than to be put on short com-
mons! It is hard to believe that Peter acted as an even more
severe overseer than the overseers of Qumran. The fact is we do
not know where St. Luke got his story about Ananias and
Sapphira. He probably found it in the traditions of the Jerusalem
Church, took it over and touched it up a bit, as was his wont,
but how far back it goes, or how it developed in the course of
transmission we have no way of telling. The utmost it tells us is

[1] Translations by Millars Borrows.
[2] Ibid.

that St. Luke himself—and presumably also the Church where he found this tradition, regarded sin against the community as a very serious thing, so much so that God was believed to have caused the deaths of this unfortunate couple. As so often in historical writing, it tells us more about the beliefs of the people who wrote it or who handed it on, than it tells us about what actually happened. In any case, the story of Ananias and Sapphira does not permit us to conclude that there was an absolutely enforced rule of communal sharing of all property.

Indeed the whole picture breaks down when we come to examine what the author of Acts writes in chapter 4. Here we read :

"The whole body of believers was united in heart and soul. Not a man of them claimed any of his possessions as his own, but everything was held in common, while the apostles bore witness with great power to the resurrection of the Lord Jesus. They were all held in high esteem; for they never had a needy person among them, because all who had property in land or houses sold it, brought the proceeds of the sale, and laid the money at the feet of the apostles; it was then distributed to any who stood in need." (Acts 4 : 32–35)

Here we seem to have a combination of two very different pictures. First, it seems to be taken for granted that there were Christians who *had* possessions, but did not claim them as their own. That is to say, they were always available for the use of any who had need of them. There was no concept of absolute ownership but rather of stewardship of wealth. But then, when we get to verse 34 we seem to be back again where we were in chapter 2, viz. with the notion that communism was the general rule : *all* who had property in land or houses sold it, brought the proceeds of the sale and laid the money at the feet of the apostles. One cannot help suspecting that the author of Acts has generalised from some specific instances. From time to time, it would appear, it happened that some particularly wealthy person realised some of his property and placed the proceeds at the disposal of the leaders of the Christian community to be used for the benefit of the poorer members. It is perhaps worth noting that in the Greek the verbs in this summary are all in the imperfect tense, which suggests that Luke is describing what he thinks was typical, rather than invariable.

Our suspicions are even more aroused when we go on to the next section. Here we are told of a particular example of one who sold his property and placed the proceeds at the disposal of the Christian leaders, viz., the case of Barnabas: "For instance, Joseph, surnamed by the apostles Barnabas (which means 'Son of Exhortation'), a Levite, by birth a Cypriot, owned an estate, which he sold; he brought the money and laid it at the apostles' feet". (Acts 4 : 36f.)

If Barnabas was simply doing what any Christian convert did, those who had property anyhow, why should his case be singled out for special mention in this way? One cannot help suspecting that the case of Barnabas, so far from being typical, was actually (exceptional—otherwise it would have never gone down on record. This means then, that Luke had before him in his sources—probably in oral rather than written traditions, though we cannot be quite sure of this—two accounts dealing with the surrender of property by Christian converts, viz., the two very different and contrasting cases of Barnabas on the one hand and Ananias and Sapphira on the other hand. From these he concluded that what was in fact an exception was actually the general rule. He then composed his summaries in Acts 2 : 44f. and 4 : 32ff., which idealise the life of the early community.

What then was the exact situation in the earliest Christian community? It is difficult to be sure, since our evidence is so scanty. But we can be sure of one or two things. First, there were the Galilean disciples who had left their daily work (e.g. fishing or tax-collecting) in order to follow Jesus. These were now the leaders of the Christian community, the apostles. A saying of Jesus was preserved in the early Church which sanctioned their receiving support from the community: "The worker earns his keep". (Matt. 10 : 10 par., Q.) Paul apparently knew of this saying, though he did not avail himself of its permission: "The Lord gave instructions that those who preach the Gospel should earn their living by the Gospel". The preservation of this saying in the early community suggests strongly that at least the apostles had to be supported by the community, which must have been a considerable burden. No doubt too—though here we have to speculate—there were other disciples who came up from Galilee to Jerusalem to join the community, and who, instead of leaving all, as the disciples apparently did, realised their property (house, farm, boat and fishing tackle, etc.) and brought the proceeds to Jerusalem. Many elderly couples retired to Jerusalem—in that respect it was like South Florida—and there would be many widows with no means of support. Finally, there would be poor Jerusalem converts who made demands on the funds available. Some of these would have been Aramaic-speaking Jewish Christians, and others Greek-speaking Jewish Christians. Barnabas was a wealthy member of the latter group. Like him, wealthy members of these two groups might realise part of their property from time to time to meet specific needs—just as a person today might realise part of his investments to meet a specific appeal, or on a humbler level, a housewife might give up all her green stamps to buy a station wagon for a community of nuns (which happened recently in Chicago area). The point about it all is that there was no hard and fast rule. As needs arose, these were met in and by the community. No one ever regarded any possessions he had as his "own" in an absolute sense. He could enjoy the use of them (responsibly, of course), but at any time a fellow Christian in need had a just claim upon them. Under certain circumstances—in the case of Barnabas, for instance, who wished to give himself to full-time work for the community —a believer could sell out all his property once for all. We may suppose that the money which came in from Barnabas and people like him helped to tide over the infant Church for a few years. But quite early on, relief programmes had to be instituted (Acts 6 : 1), while the famines of the forties accentuated the problem and gave rise to the Pauline collection, which will be discussed in the next chapter.

What then are we to make of all this? Certain points stand out. First, the early Christians did not believe that God was only interested in a man's spiritual relation with Him. *Koinonia* with God involved also *koinonia* with one's fellow-believers. Closely connected with this was the refusal to draw a sharp distinction between the spiritual and the material, between what we would call the sacred and the secular, or between religion and life. In the exercise of Christian love it was necessary to concern oneself—albeit on what from our standpoint looks like a very primitive, elementary level—with material goods. The use of goods provided the concrete context in which the demand of love could be met. Finally there is a very *ad hoc* attitude towards all this. There was no hard and fast rule for everyone at all times. The early community's rule was *solvitur ambulando,* or in the good old British way, to "muddle through", to meet concrete situations as they arose. First, the wealthy realised their possessions from time to time to meet the growing needs of the poor. Then, a bit later, the relief programme had to be organised on a more systematic basis (Acts 6 : 1ff.). For it is the concrete situation that provides the context in which Christian obedience has to be worked out. We shall study another of the concrete situations in the following chapter.

4

PAUL AND THE COLLECTION FOR THE JERUSALEM CHURCH

THERE was a profound difference between the original Jerusalem Church and the Churches of the Gentile mission, whose head-quarters were in Antioch. The original Christians remained devout Jews, keeping the Jewish law. The mission from Antioch (itself a mixed Church consisting partly of Jewish [Greek-speaking] Christians, and partly of Gentiles) resulted in the foundation of predominantly Gentile Churches. These Christians were admitted to the Church without any requirement that they should keep the Jewish law. Apparently as yet no one had raised the question. In particular, no demand was imposed upon them that they should be circumcised.

But there were some rigid Jewish Christians at Jerusalem who did not approve of all this. Some of them—"sham Christians" and "interlopers" Paul calls them—came down to Antioch and "stole in to spy upon the liberty we enjoy in the fellowship of Christ Jesus".[1] (Gal. 2 : 4; cf. Acts 15 : 1) "Certain persons who had come down from Judea began to teach the brotherhood that those who were not circumcised in accordance with Mosaic practice could not be saved." As a result and in accordance with a revelation (perhaps the revelation of a prophet who said that they ought to go), Paul and Barnabas went up to Jerusalem. They went as the representatives of the Antioch Church and its mission, taking along with them Titus, a Gentile Greek. The issue was so critical that it could only be settled at the highest level.

[1] Throughout this account I follow Gal. 2 : 1ff., exclusively. The traditions behind the accounts of this visit in Acts 11, 12 and 15 are thoroughly confused. As always when there is a conflict between Acts and Paul, Paul must be followed since his is a first hand account and is written much closer to the events. At the same time we have to make allowances for the immediate purpose for which Paul is writing. Luke's account is written in good faith, but at a distance, and his combines traditions of different events or duplicates two or more traditions of the same event. Luke's writing tells us much more about his own outlook and the interests of the Church in his day than it does about the events he is narrating.

A summit conference had to be held. It was however a private meeting between Paul and Barnabas on the one hand, and the leaders of the Jerusalem Church on the other. Paul refers to them as "men of repute" (Gal. 2 : 2), "men of high reputation" (v. 6), "the reputed pillars of our society" (v. 9). They were James, the brother of the Lord, Cephas (i.e. Peter) and John the son of Zebedee. Our first impression is that Paul is belittling their authority, and speaking of their reputation ironically. Especially does this seem to be the case in verse 6 where he adds in parenthesis, "not that their importance matters to me : God does not recognise these personal distinctions". But Paul certainly recognised their authority as apostles. This is clear when he says that it was "God whose action made Peter an apostle to the Jews" (v. 8). There he clearly recognises Peter's authority. Paul's words about the pillars, the men of repute, etc., reflect the language his later opponents in Galatia were employing. These later opponents exalted the authority of the Jerusalem leaders for the wrong reasons. At this private meeting, Paul tells us, he laid before the Jerusalem leaders the Gospel he was accustomed to preach among the Gentiles. In particular, we may suppose, he stressed that he never required his converts to submit to circumcision. Would the Jerusalem Church recognise the preaching of the Gospel without the requirement of circumcision? Everything was at stake here. If they did not, Paul (and Barnabas, and the Church at Antioch) would have "run in vain"—that is to say, his whole work as an apostle and missionary would have been destroyed. For it was the purpose of the Gospel to gather all men into unity in Christ, and if the Jerusalem authorities rejected— as the false brethren, the sham Christians, were trying to force them to do—then there would not be one Church, but two, one Jewish and one Gentile. That would be a denial of Christ, a denial of the Gospel, and a denial of its effects. So what is at stake at this conference is Christian unity—the unity of the Gospel, the unity of the apostolic ministry, and the unity of the Church.

Apparently some of the sham Christians wormed their way into the conference and tried to make Titus a test case. Let Paul, if he means business, they demanded, have Titus circumcised. If he does that, then we can recognise him and his Gospel. Was Paul prepared to make this concession? No doubt that question was put to him by the pillars. But Paul dug his toes in. He refused to have Titus circumcised and no doubt explained why—the whole Gospel was once more at stake. Salvation is the gift of God in Christ alone, offered freely through faith in His grace, not by the works of the law. The pillars were apparently convinced, for Titus was not compelled to be circumcised. The pressure was dropped, and Paul had won the immediate issue. But there was still the wider issue, the policy of the Gentile mission in the field. This was speedily settled. The "men of repute did not prolong the consultation, but on the contrary acknowledged that I had been entrusted with the Gospel for Gentiles as Peter had been entrusted with the Gospel for Jews".

Paul writes as though it were only his personal position which was at stake. He seems to forget Barnabas for the moment, and even more the whole Antioch Church and its mission, which he was representing. This is because he was at this time writing to the Galatians, wherein his own personal authority as an apostle was being criticised. But really, it was not just Paul's personal authority which was being recognised at the Jerusalem conference, but the whole policy of the Antioch mission to the Gentiles. When he comes to the conclusion of the consultation, he suddenly remembers that Barnabas was there, and also that at this time Barnabas was his superior as the representative of the Church at Antioch, for he puts Barnabas first in verse 9 :

"Recognising, then, the favour thus bestowed upon me, (the pillars) accepted *Barnabas and myself* as partners, and shook hands upon it, agreeing that we should go to the Gentiles while they went to the Jews."

This is the celebrated "gentlemen's agreement". It does not mean that there were to be two different geographical areas, one taken over by Peter and the other by Paul. Nor can it have meant in practice that there were two distinct missions, in which Peter concentrated exclusively on converting Jews and Paul on the Gentiles. We know in fact that Peter later appeared in areas which were covered by Paul. Soon after he appeared in Antioch (Gal. 2 : 11) at the same time as Paul. He may have been at

Corinth, for he certainly enjoyed some influence there (I Cor. 1 : 12, etc.). And the tradition that he ended up in Rome (where Paul also ended up) and died a martyr's death is early and fairly strong.

We gather too from Paul's letters ("to the Jew first, and then to the Greek") that he did not regard himself as prohibited from working among Jews. Rather, the gentlemen's agreement recognises the main direction of Peter's work and Paul's. Peter was to concentrate mainly on the Jews and Paul on the Gentiles. As a result, the Churches founded by Peter would be mainly Jewish communities, where the law would be kept, while the communities founded by Paul would consist mainly, if not exclusively, of Gentiles. There the Gentile converts would be entirely free of the Jewish law. Nevertheless they were still one Church, and this unity was to be given concrete and practical expression. This was the only string attached to the gentlemen's agreement :

"All that they asked was that we should keep their poor in mind, which was the very thing I made it my business to do." (Gal. 2 : 10) Here at last we come to the important point for our interest. Although the immediate issue—whether the Gentile converts should be circumcised—is now one which is dead and done with, perhaps precisely because it was settled at this very conference—the broader issues it raised are ever with us. First, there was the question of agreement in the truth of the Gospel. In our pragmatic age, and particularly in a not overly doctrinal Church like the Anglican communion, we tend to ignore the importance of agreement over the truth of the Gospel as the primary basis of inter-communion. (How quickly in ecumenical conferences and in inter-church relationships do we reach doctrinal agreements, and how stubborn is our insistence on episcopacy; how little do the creeds—to say nothing of the Thirty-nine Articles—figure in our discussions. Here is something we must learn from our Lutheran brethren.) But the question of agreement in the truth of the Gospel—which was primary—does lead to the second question, the question of the mutual recognition of ministries. This depends on two things : first, agreement about the truth of the Gospel. Secondly, that the minister should have been properly entrusted with his ministry

D

by God ("I had been entrusted"—God entrusted me—as He had entrusted Peter with his apostleship). Unity in the truth of the Gospel, followed by mutual recognition of ministry at once leads to the integration of the two parts of the missions—they solemnly shook hands upon it. But then what? A programme of mutual responsibility and interdependence! Here, at the Jerusalem conference is launched the first M.R.I. programme in the Church's history! It wasn't invented at Toronto or first heard of in 1963!

Not indeed that the gentlemen's agreement took exactly the same form as the current M.R.I. programme. It was tailored to meet the needs of the concrete situation. The Jerusalem Church was the mother church of the growing number of Christians throughout the Mediterranean area. From Jerusalem the Gospel had sounded forth into all lands. That was the mother church's main contribution to M.R.I. But the Jerusalem Church itself was poor. There were many poor members there, and in the previous chapter we saw the reason why. Not that the Gentile Churches of the Antioch mission were at all affluent by our present-day standards. But at least they consisted of people who continued to reside in the cities where they were converted to Christianity. They hadn't, like the Galileans, abandoned their places of work to go up to Jerusalem and wait for the second coming. So here was a concrete need, and it was met by an *ad hoc* answer.

IMPLEMENTING THE PROGRAMME

The Jerusalem conference was probably held in the year A.D. 49. We hear nothing further of the plan to make a collection for the Jerusalem poor until Paul's first (surviving) letter to the Corinthians, written some time after A.D. 52 (the year he left Corinth after his first visit there, when he founded the Church). When he wrote I Corinthians he took up a number of points raised by the Corinthians in a letter they had sent to him (I Cor. 7:1, 25, 8:1, 12:1). The question of the collection was the last on the list of these questions (I Cor. 16:1). Evidently, Paul had already broached the matter, either on his original visit, or in an earlier letter he had written to the Corinthians. This letter is now lost, but is alluded to in I Corinthians

5 : 9. The Corinthians have evidently raised two questions about the collection : (1) How was the money to be raised? (2) How was the sum collected to be taken up to Jerusalem? Paul answers both these points in I Corinthians 16 : 1-4, which we will quote at length :

"And now about the collection in aid of God's people: you should follow my directions to our congregations in Galatia. Every Sunday each of you is to put aside and keep by him a sum in proportion to his gains, so that there may be no collecting when I come. When I arrive, I will give letters of introduction to persons approved by you, and send them to carry your gift to Jerusalem. If it should seem worth while for me to go as well, they shall go with me."

Paul makes some very interesting points here. He wants their giving to be regular and systematic. He does not want to whip round with the plate when he comes, perhaps rousing their emotions by an eloquent sermon. Every Sunday each of the faithful is to set aside a carefully-calculated amount, proportionate to his earnings during the previous week. For us perhaps it is a little surprising that Paul did not suggest that they should bring their offering to church and put it in the Sunday collection. The Sunday collection is not mentioned until Justin Martyr (c. 150). Nowadays the Corinthian wardens might even have invested the money temporarily until Paul was ready to take receipt of it. Unfortunately, such opportunities do not appear to have been open in those days! It is particularly interesting to see that Paul recommends *proportionate* giving. God and one's fellow Christians, he suggests, have a claim to a proportionate share of one's income. Christians are stewards, not absolute owners of their wealth. Wisely, perhaps, he does not lay down a law of tithing, but leaves each member of the Church to decide on the proportion. Tithing would be hard on the poorer members, while the rich could no doubt have given more. Also he insists that *everyone* should give ("each one of you"). This is the first every-member canvas!

Paul leaves open whether he will accompany the delegates when they go up to Jerusalem with the gift. It will depend on the amount raised. If it is sufficiently impressive, Paul will go along with it. For then the gift will have a special significance. What that significance will be he does not mention here, but it will become clear in his later letters when he takes up the subject again.

Paul's every-member canvas at Corinth got off to a good start. It seems that the Corinthians laid their plans with great enthusiasm. He was able to hold them up as an example to his other Churches; those in Macedonia: "I know how eager you are to help; I speak of it with pride to the Macedonians: I tell them that Achaia had everything ready last year; and most of them have been fired by your zeal." (II Cor. 9 : 2) But Paul was a bit over-optimistic. There's many a slip 'twixt cup and lip. Unfortunately new and unforeseen troubles flared up at Corinth, which led to a year's delay in the fund-raising drive. False teachers turned up at Corinth and made a sharp attack on Paul's authority as an apostle. We hear about this in the "severe letter" of II Corinthians 10–13. They accused Paul of moral weakness (II Cor. 10 : 2). "His letters", they said, "are weighty and powerful, but when he appears he has no presence, and as a speaker he is beneath contempt." (v. 10) These "superlative apostles", as Paul ironically dubs them, these "sham apostles", crooked in all their practices, masquerading as apostles of Christ (II Cor. 11 : 5, 13) brought with them "another gospel" (11 : 4). He does not tell us directly what that gospel was but reading between the lines we gather that it presented Christ not as the One who was crucified in weakness, who died to justify the ungodly, but as a spectacular wonder-worker. They vaunted their own apostleship. They boasted that they were able to produce such spectacular miracles, visions, ecstasies, etc. as Christ did. Thus they showed a spirit very different from the Spirit of Christ, which frees a man from self-love for love of neighbour. The susceptible Corinthians, who in Paul's first letter already were clearly prone to emphasise such showy gifts of the Spirit as speaking in tongues and miracles rather than Christian love (that is the whole point of Paul's celebrated hymn to charity in I Corinthians 13!), quickly fell for the sham teachers and their specious claims: "How gladly you bear with fools, being yourselves so wise!" (II Cor. 11 : 19)

Faced with this apparently successful challenge to his own authority as an apostle, and indeed to the very Gospel itself, Paul left Ephesus and paid a lightning visit to his erring flock. This visit is alluded to in II Corinthians 2:1 and 13:1. Evidently it was a complete fiasco—a "painful" visit, Paul calls it. It was this fiasco that brought the charge already noted, that "when he [Paul] appears he has no presence". Balked on this occasion, Paul returned to Ephesus with his tail between his legs and tried a different tack. He would write them a severe letter—since his letters apparently were so much more effective than his presence —and send it by Titus, his trusted henchman. So he penned II Corinthians 10–13, written, as he later recalls, under great emotion: "That letter I sent you came out of great distress and anxiety; how many tears I shed as I wrote it!" (II Cor. 2:4) Point by point he goes over the false claims of the sham apostles and the charges they had levelled against him. And in answer he stresses not his eloquence, his visions, his Jewish ancestry, his works of wonder (all the things the false apostles gloried in), but his apostolic labours: "I can outdo them. More overworked than they, scourged more severely, more often imprisoned, many a time face to face with death. Five times the Jews have given me the thirty-nine strokes; three times I have been beaten with rods; once I was stoned; three times I have been shipwrecked, and for twenty-four hours I was adrift on the open sea. I have been constantly on the road; I have met dangers from rivers, dangers from my fellow-countrymen, dangers from foreigners, dangers in towns, dangers in the country, dangers at sea, dangers from false friends. I have toiled and drudged, I have often gone without sleep; hungry and thirsty, I have often gone fasting; and I have suffered from cold and exposure." (II Cor. 11: 23–27) In all this Paul is emphasising what the false apostles had no time for—the Gospel message of the Cross, and a life conformed to the Cross.

What, meanwhile, of the every-member canvas? For the time being it was wrecked. Collecting for the saints at Jerusalem was something for which the Corinthians now had no time. That sort of thing was far too humdrum when they had all the excitements offered by the sham apostles—miracles, visions, ecstasies

and all the rest of it. Religion had come to be for them something for selfish enjoyment—not "being for others", not the way
of the Cross. In any case, the whole idea of the collection was
Paul's scheme, and Paul was in bad odour just then.

It was touch and go between Paul and the Corinthians. It took
the severe letter and all the diplomacy Titus could muster to
bring them round again to their senses. It was a long drawn out
business, and Paul was nearly beside himself with anxiety. He
left Ephesus for Troas. Still Titus did not come. Eventually Paul
could stand it no longer, and went to Macedonia, where at last
Titus turned up with the good news that all was well again
II Cor. 2 : 12f., 7 : 5ff.). The Corinthians had expelled the sham
apostles, so Paul pens off a letter full of joy and a sense of relief
(II Cor. 1–9). Having expressed at length his thankfulness that
the crisis was over, he turns again to something that had been in
his mind all along—the collection! (II Cor. 8–9). One by one he
marshals every conceivable argument in support of his fund-
raising drive. No wonder Archbishop Cranmer turned to these
chapters for his offertory sentences in the Communion service!
Let us list them :

1. Think how well the Macedonians have done in *their* fund-
raising drive! They are a poor community, yet they have gone
to the limit of their resources and even beyond the limit (II Cor.
8 : 1ff.).

2. Compared with the Macedonians, the Corinthians are
affluent. How much more lavish ought *they* to be over the collection ! (v. 7).

3. A theological argument : "Christ became poor for your
sakes that you might become rich". Therefore they must show
their gratitude for the Gospel by Christian giving (v. 9).

4. A reminder of the good start they had made a year ago :
"be as eager to complete the scheme as you were to adopt it, and
give according to your means" (v. 11).

5. The mutual interdependence between the Churches. At the
moment, the Corinthians have superfluity of abundance, so they
ought to share with the Jerusalem Christians, to equalise things
out (vv. 12–15).

6. A cunning reversal of argument No. 1 : Paul has been boasting of the Corinthians' generosity to the Macedonians, so they must not let him down! (9 : 1–5).

7. It pays to be generous. The point is driven home by some familiar proverbs (vv. 6–10).

8. The spiritual benefits the Corinthians will receive from the recipients. There will be a "flood of thanksgiving to God" (vv. 11–12). The Jerusalem Church will pray for the Corinthians and their hearts will go out to them (v. 14).

So, in anticipation, Paul closes with the memorable exclamation : "Thanks be to God for his gift beyond words!".

Probably the most important aspect of this whole discussion with the Corinthians is that Paul sets the collection for the saints at Jerusalem in the context of the main issue that had dogged all his dealings with the Church at Corinth—namely, the subject of the "charismata" or spiritual gifts. The Corinthians shared with the contemporary pagan world the belief that supernatural phenomena—ecstasies, visions, miracles and the like, were the supreme manifestations of the Spirit. Paul will not quench these gifts of the Spirit, but he insists that they must be put to the test. Not the supernatural as such is good and holy and divine—it may even be the work of evil spirits and the demons. It all depends on whether these supernatural gifts spring from the confession of Jesus as Lord, as the crucified One who justifies the ungodly. Where this is the case, the gifts will be used in the service of the community for its upbuilding, for the purposes of Christian love (agape). Indeed, it does not really matter in the last analysis whether a Christian congregation manifests the supernatural phenomena (even speaking with tongues, which is increasing among Episcopalians in the U.S.A., and as report has it is getting under way in England too) or not. There is a more excellent way, the way of agape, of Christian love, which can be present, even where the supernatural phenomena are absent. Indeed, as Paul constantly warns the Corinthians, the supernatural phenomena are often inimical to agape, for they lead to self-sufficiency and pride, instead of to "being for others". Within the congregation itself

Christian love expresses itself in its concern for the weaker brethren whom the more "spiritual" members of the community (those with the spectacular gifts) are tempted to despise: "Love is kind and envies no one. Love is never boastful, nor conceited, nor rude; never selfish, not quick to take offence. Love keeps no score of wrongs; does not gloat over sins, but delights in the truth." (I Cor. 13 :6f.) But there is another dimension of Christian love. This dimension is the relation between one local Christian community and another, between the local Christian community and the world-wide Church. The Christians at Corinth were sorely tempted to a false congregationalism. They imagined that they were the only church in the world. Again and again Paul has to remind them that they were but a part of a much greater, wider fellowship.

Right at the start of his first letter he reminds them that they are "the congregation of God's people at Corinth". They are not just the sole congregation of God's people. There are congregations of the one people of God in other places besides Corinth. The Corinthian congregation is not a self-sufficient religious club, but one of many local manifestations of the One Holy People of God. And they are precisely the people *of God*— not constituted by their own religiousness, their own spectacular gifts and experiences. And they are all of them "dedicated to God in Christ Jesus, claimed by him as his own"—literally "sanctified, or made holy, in Christ Jesus, called to be saints". *All* of them are this—not just the gifted few, but all who have been baptised. For their holiness depends solely on the act of God in Christ, who justifies the ungodly in baptism. Their false congregationalism is further broken down with the words which follow: "along with all men everywhere who invoke the name of our Lord Jesus Christ—their Lord as well as ours". Although Paul does not allude to the collection until the end of the letter, this insistence of the Corinthians' membership of a much wider fellowship than their own local congregation provides the theological basis for that expression of mutual responsibility and interdependence. The same reminder of this universal fellowship to which they belong is repeated from time to time in the body of the first letter. When he speaks of sending Timothy to

them, he says: "He will remind you of the way of life I follow,
and which I teach *everywhere in all our congregations*". His
teaching is not a special teaching for the Corinthians alone, but
the common faith of all the churches. Christian doctrine is not
something which wells up as it were out of the experience of a
particular congregation, as would be the case if the Church were
just a religious club. It is precisely the *Catholic* faith, in the true
sense of the word. Similarly, in his discussion of the ethics of
marriage and sex he reminds them: "That is what I teach *in
all our congregations*". (I Cor. 7:17) And again, when dealing
with abuses in worship he sternly remarks: "However, if you
insist on arguing, let me tell you, there is no such custom among
us, *or in any of the congregations of God's people*". (I Cor.
11:16) Then later, in a similar vein, and again in discussing the
goings-on in the worship at Corinth, he exclaims indignantly,
"Did the word of God originate with you? Or are you the only
people to whom it came?". (I Cor. 14:36) Although Paul does
not say so here, this is precisely why he insisted on the collection
for the saints at Jerusalem. The word of God did not originate
at Corinth. It came first to the Church at Jerusalem, and therefore the Corinthians are bound to them by the ties of mutual
responsibility and interdependence.

The last we hear from Paul about his collection is in his letter
to the Romans. This was written from Corinth—or from the
port of Cenchreae near Corinth—just before his departure for
Jerusalem. He explains to the Romans that he has finished his
missionary work in the eastern Mediterranean, and is anxious to
come and see them on his way to Spain. "But at the moment I
am on my way to Jerusalem, on an errand to God's people there.
For Macedonia and Achaia have resolved to raise a common
fund for the benefit of the poor among God's people at Jerusalem." (Rom. 15:25f.) Now at last he gives us what he has not
done before, a succinct statement of the purpose which underlay
the whole scheme of the fund-raising campaign: "For if the
Jewish Christians shared their spiritual treasures with the
Gentiles, the Gentiles have a clear duty to contribute to their
material needs." For it was at Jerusalem that the mighty acts of

God had taken place—the passion and death of Jesus Christ, his resurrection,[1] the outpouring of the spirit and the first preaching of the Gospel. That is why Paul had so readily agreed at the Jerusalem conference to undertake the collection for the saints. It was the "clear duty" of the Gentiles, and once they had rightly come to understand the true nature of the Gospel (so threatened at Corinth by the appearance of the sham apostles) they buckled down and made the collection as a free-will offering. So Paul is now looking forward to his trip to Jerusalem to "finish this business and deliver the proceeds under his own seal". He had said earlier (I Cor. 16 : 4, see above) that he would only go up in person "if he thought it worthwhile". Evidently the amount collected was so impressive that it certainly was worthwhile for him to go up in person. As the head of the mission to the Gentiles he will appear in Jerusalem as a living witness to the unity of the Church. It is not enough for the unity of the Church to be expressed in the sharing of spiritual things—in the Gospel—or, in our day, the vessels in which the treasure of the Gospel is preserved and conveyed, scripture, creeds, liturgy, sacraments and a commonly-recognised ministry.[2]

Paul's collection, like the earlier sharing of goods in the original Jerusalem community, is an expression of Christian *koinonia*, but in changed circumstances. There is no final law in the Church as to the precise form the expression of *koinonia* must take. That must depend on the given circumstances of the moment. But of one thing we can be sure. Wherever the Church exists, there will be this *koinonia*—a common sharing in the spiritual gifts of the Gospel. But, too, wherever the Church exists, this spiritual *koinonia*, if it is genuine, will always be given material expression, in terms of dollars and cents, of pounds,

---

[1] One cannot really locate the resurrection, for it takes place at the point of intersection between time and eternity. Modern scholars are uncertain as to the precise location of the resurrection appearances. Probably the earliest ones (to Peter and the Twelve, 1 Cor. 15 : 5) took place in Galilee, but some of the later ones must have taken place in Jerusalem, and in any case the first witnesses of the resurrection soon returned from Galilee to Jerusalem, and it was there that they launched their preaching of the death and resurrection of Jesus.

[2] The Anglican reader will recognise the allusion to the Lambeth-Chicago quadrilateral, but the liturgy has been added as a fifth bond of unity in the Gospel, as F. D. Maurice, the ultimate originator of the quadrilateral, intended.

shillings and pence. Affluence must therefore be seen, as Paul would see it, as a charisma, a gift of the Spirit. But, like the spectacular gifts in the Church at Corinth, affluence is a double-edged thing. It can be used for selfish enjoyment—whether of the individual or of the particular congregation (today expressed in ever bigger church building programmes). Then it becomes no better than that phenomenon of affluence in the pagan world, the spiritual gifts at Corinth. But if affluence is under-stood genuinely as a charisma, a gift to faithful believers in the Gospel of the crucified and risen Lord who justifies the ungodly, then it becomes a charisma, a gift of grace, and is used as such. It is used in the service of the community. To quote some words of a contemporary German New Testament scholar (Ernst Käseman) written in a discussion of the charismata at Corinth which, as we have seen, is not unconnected in that letter with the notion of affluence :

"The true measure of this gift is the way in which, in and for the Lord, an existing set of circumstances is transformed; that is, it is the obedience of a Christian man. . . . My previous condition of life becomes charisma only when I recognise that the Lord has given it to me and that I am able to accept this gift as his calling and command to me. Now everything can become for me charisma (including, we might add, affluence). It would be not only foolish but a slight to the honour of Christ, who wills to fill all things, if I were to attempt to take the realms of the natural, the sexual, the private, the social, out of His sphere of power. . . . All things stand within the charismatic possibility and are holy to the extent to which the holy ones of God make use of them." [1] Here, in Paul's teaching on the charismata, we see the high water mark of the New Testament's teaching on affluence.

[1] *Essays on New Testament Themes*, 1964, p. 72.

PART TWO

WEALTH IN MODERN SOCIETY

BY BRIAN K. RICE

5

ALL GOOD GIFTS

THIS discussion is a Transatlantic venture. Both writers have lived and worked in America and in Britain. We are here seeking to relate our biblical studies to the remaining years of the twentieth century; and it is this world around us which forms the second half of our enquiry.

Each one of us has our own views about the nineteen-sixties, our own circumstances, evidence and experience. Some think we live in an age of prosperity; others think that these are still days of comparative hardship and poverty. We all think that other people are well off and that we deserve much more prosperity than we have. This may make us less sympathetic towards other sections of the community, and we must beware of this possibility.

The sixties and seventies are presenting a special challenge to Christians on both sides of the Atlantic. Ordinary folks are more directly involved in social affairs, economics and politics than at any previous time in history. Prosperity is a good thing, but it causes many serious problems. We have long suspected that the problem of affluence and Christian responsibility may be a blind spot for many. This is the concern of the whole community and therefore cannot be neglected by the people of God.

Christ was among us as a "sign" and our immediate concern is to open up two particular questions. What are the "signs" of the times, and in what sense are Christians called to be "signs" in the sixties?

Why are such enquiries imperative? Because "God so loved the world"—not the faithful, not the Church, but the world, this world around us. *This world*—with its rising prosperity, its starving millions, its criminals, its mentally sick, its lonely, its juvenile delinquents, its bigness—is ever God's world. He is Father of the affluent society. Christ died for the nineteen-sixties. This is the definition of the relation of the Church to our world of prosperity: this summons us to dialogue. Too often the Church seems to be engaged only in monologue, in talking to itself about itself.

At this point it is wise to remember that politics and economics were practised well and badly long before Christianity came into the world. Not only does this fact demonstrate the ease with which Christians should be able to co-operate with others, but it urges us to refrain from the habit of assuming that all good action is inspired by religion. Clearly in countries which have been Christianised for centuries, our ideas of right and wrong must be profoundly affected by Christian influence. But this does not allow us to claim natural virtues like honesty, compassion, or justice as belonging exclusively or even predominantly to Christians.

Both writers were at Peterhouse, Cambridge, and we commend these words of the present Master, Professor Herbert Butterfield: "I cannot say that in history statesmanship works under entirely different laws if a politician happens to be a Christian or even a clergyman—if politics are influenced, say, by a Wolsey or a Laud. I cannot say, looking over the centuries, that the clergy seem to me to have been always right against the laity, at any rate in the conflicts that pertain to mundane affairs. I think that in modern centuries the unbeliever has sometimes even fought the churchman for what we today would regard as the higher ethical end, the one which most corresponds with the deeper influences of Christianity."

For priests to undertake discussion of the social scene, political issues and economic affairs, is usually looked on with some suspicion—perhaps quite rightly! If these are thought of as dirty business, this is all the more reason for Christians to be in the midst of things. William Temple warned: "The claim of the Christian Church to make its voice heard in matters of politics and economics is very widely resented, even by those who are Christian in personal belief and devotional practice. It is commonly assumed that religion is one department of life, like art or science, and that it is playing the part of a busybody when it lays down principles for the guidance of other departments, whether art and science or business and politics." And we may

affirm with Archbishop Temple that it is "the right and duty of
the Church to declare its judgment upon social facts and social
movements and to lay down principles which should govern the
ordering of society". But how is this to be done?

The affluent society is more than a slogan. It expresses enormous change in the way people live. Better housing, better saving,
better domestic appliances, better cars, better working conditions,
and more of all these things. They are no longer confined to a
privileged minority but belong to most of the population. The
first cost of living index in Britain prepared by the Board of
Trade in 1900 did not even include butter or electricity, as these
were not considered part of any normal working-class budget;
the latest index, prepared in 1962, makes allowances for washing-
machines and T.V. sets. This is a good thing and there seems
every reason to believe that with increasing economic productivity these improvements will continue and spread. And the
Church is in the midst of prosperity, very wealthy in manpower,
money and market-potential.

We can be too optimistic. Professor Galbraith's book *The
Affluent Society* (1958) dealt almost exclusively with the American scene. No other country approaches the standards of living
of the U.S., even though in America there is still widespread
poverty and unemployment. The output per head in manufacturing industries in this country is only half that in the
States, largely because American industry is so much more
highly mechanised than British—the horse-power used per
worker is twice as great in U.S. factories as in British factories.
When Galbraith "initiated" the affluent society he was not
referring to this country, and in America there is still much
hardship even though his analysis appeared almost a decade ago.

For other reasons also, we must not be too optimistic. In spite
of all the progress that has been achieved in material ways, there
has probably never been a period in the history of mankind
when there has been so much fear and insecurity—fear of war,
fear of poverty, fear of unemployment, fear of nuclear destruction. Hence the constant strikes for higher wages, the wave of
speculation in shares and in property, the urge to "get rich

E

quick" even at the expense of friends and neighbours, the H.P. debts, the gambling craze, the exploitation of young people by commercial interests. These activities tend to deny human dignity and self-respect, yet few seem to recognise that the Christian answer can only be effective if it takes account of the economic motives behind them.

Hardship does exist today. It has not been abolished, but it has been reduced in remarkable ways. Certainly it is less widespread and less severe today than for our parents and grandparents. Probably we shall never avoid hardship in an affluent society because it is a comparative state. Some will always earn more than others. *In any case, low wages or pensions are not the only cause of hardship—unless we forget crime, suicide, divorce, sickness, accident, vice and the like.*

The things which are flourishing amidst our prosperity are venereal disease, mental disorder, bad debts, juvenile delinquency, drug addiction, strikes, bankruptcy, suicide and crime. And these "signs of the times" are world-wide. We seldom love our present possessions. We must have more. We adore the things we do not own and look down to them as a source of happiness. Almost everyone is affected by this point of view. Most of us accept without question the idea that if only we owned things which we do not have, we should be much happier and more content.

Prosperity is forcing Christians to face major issues. So far we have tended to turn away and ignore the existence of such problems. We cannot go on turning a blind eye: many of these problems are now at the door of every home in the land. They are not isolated, but interdependent, and they influence us day by day. Redundancies involve homes . . . mental patients involve homes . . . nuclear weapons involve homes . . . strikes involve homes. . . . People make society affluent or otherwise; herein is the significance of the individual. God created us individually to live together. And it is the general insecurity of the world around us which heightens the personal insecurity of each of us. We see tensions in the external world which are indicative of many strains within man himself. A noted psychiatrist, Dr. C. J. Jung, was once asked by one of his patients: "Dr.

Jung, how do you keep your patience with us and our puny problems when Europe is falling apart and you have work of world importance?". Jung replied: "Because the world problems start with individuals". He went on to describe the aimless hesitations of Western civilisation: "Side by side with the decline of religious life", he says, "the neuroses grow noticeably more frequent. Everywhere the mental state of men shows an alarming lack of balance. We are living undoubtedly in a period of great restlessness, nervous tension, confusion and disorientation of outlook. . . . Everyone has the feeling that our modern religious truths have somehow or other grown empty."

Our discussion starts and ends with individuals, with our opportunities and problems. Ideally we should each make our own diagnosis of the nineteen-sixties. Invariably this will be a spiral rather than a straight line, near pattern or exact formula. Our survey is incomplete and not original and we are probably most interested in those aspects of affluence which vex the Christian, aspects which make life easier materially but more difficult in other ways. Doubtless we have our own blindspots and presuppositions!

We seek to discuss the affluent society as it challenges the people of God and in its setting in biblical theology. Our survey is an attempt to gather together facts and figures to enable Christians to reassess our affluence in the light of Christ. Such a survey is too brief to present all the evidence at our disposal, let alone attempt to evaluate it meaningfully. But it may act as a stimulant to further prayer, thought and action. Of course average figures have their strict limitations. Vast statistics can become meaningless unless they are set within a specific context.

It will be obvious that we entertain no special claim to see into the future. No one can foretell what 1967–68 has in store for mankind. It is not possible to assess the situation in South-East Asia six months hence, for example, or whether the U.S. economy will level off in 1967, or how drastically the United Kingdom "credit squeeze" and heavier taxation will cut back productivity and increase unemployment. *No one knows whether we shall even get to 1970—or whether Viet-nam will have produced World War Three and nuclear destruction.* Some of our present enquiries are bound to be out of date quickly—just as tomorrow's headlines are always dated by tonight's television news coverage.

Figures quoted here are as accurate as possible, and are the latest available in America and Britain, revised Spring 1966. But they are not intended to *prove* anything. They are set down to indicate *trends* in daily life. Just one example at random : on the front page of the *Financial Times* this morning was the number of Britain's births last year—873,990 babies. On another page was the number of new vehicles registered in Britain in the same year—1,710,332. Obviously this does not *prove* that every family who had a baby last year also bought a new car : it does, however, indicate a *trend* in our prosperity, namely that the output of new cars (1,192,412) is now 30 per cent higher than the birth rate and that thousands of families can afford to spend £500–£1000 on a new car, plus £3–4 *every week* on running it. It now takes a motorist 36½ weeks' wages to buy a car, or 30 weeks excluding purchase tax, compared with 65 weeks' wages in 1938.

There are other implications of new cars. A similar number— almost a million—were exported in 1965. This is a major industry on both sides of the Atlantic, involving millions of homes. America has (almost) one car for every two inhabitants, but there are numerous three- and four-car families, which means that there are still a few households which do not possess this supreme status symbol. University of Michigan researchers said Americans spent a record of £7500 million to buy 9 million new cars in 1965. How long can this rate of progress continue ? Earlier this year "one of the largest surveys ever attempted in the world" covered 3 million homes in Britain. It showed that two families in every five have a car and one household in 10 has more than one car. The national average is 5.8 people per car. If the present rate of vehicle ownership continues until the year 2000—only 30 years hence—*everyone on average will own between two and three vehicles and each household will have 10.*

New cars are only one of many trends in the midst of prosperity. The family car is a welcome asset, but cars—like families —are not without their problems. The few facts mentioned give some indication of tension as well as blessings, and we have said nothing about road congestion, accidents, parking; nothing about strikes, automation, redundancy in the motor industry. These are part of prosperity, they involve homes and people. The new car is a sign of the times, a good thing : but it would be sub-Christian to ignore its implications. We cannot say that new cars—to give only one example—are an unqualified blessing on society. Too many new cars *do* raise problems. Buyers of new American cars will have to pay a "burial fee" of up to £18 to cover the final disposal of the car if a proposal being studied by the House of Representatives Sub-Committee on Roads becomes law. Americans now change their cars every three years on average and the Government is seeking ways to eradicate the unsightly roadside graveyards of old and wrecked cars. There are now 18,726 car scrapheaps and junk-yards alongside the main roads of America. The "trash" business is the fastest growing industry in the U.S. Car-breakers are buying 1959–60 cars for £3–4 for breaking up, cars which originally cost £1000 plus. In Britain some 400,000 wrecked and worn-out cars are left on the roads each year; and mobile car-crushers can now crush and bundle a complete car every $1\frac{1}{2}$ minutes into a block measuring 11 × 22 × 24 inches. Certainly too many new cars are raising serious problems : in 1966 poor sales are already closing some U.S. car plants (A.M.C. is 31 per cent down on 1965).

There is no Christian objection to prosperity. On the contrary : Christ claimed that He came that we might have life and have it more abundantly. All good gifts around us are sent from heaven above, we sing. "I was glad" says the psalmist "that their corn and oil and wine increased." The good things of life are gifts of God to be enjoyed, and the good things of our prosperous society can be very good indeed.

Take, for instance, the often-quoted symbols of television, washing-machines and refrigerators. Television can unite the family in a common interest, can transport the sick and the elderly out of the confines of their physical situation, and can educate us all into new knowledge and new understanding. Domestic appliances save endless drudgery, preserve food, make new forms of cooking possible, make kitchens healthy and living-rooms delightful.

All these things—and with them good clothes, good food, good holidays, good housing—are materials which surely God wants His children to enjoy. Man can be helped by the good things of affluence: he can be hindered by the bad things of poverty. It is the "cares of this world" equally with the deceitfulness of riches that prevent the growth of the good seed. The fact of affluence itself does not make people better: it only gives us increased opportunities of being and doing so.

This applies to churches and to nations no less than to individuals. All alike will be judged by the opportunities that are ours and the uses we make of them. If in the Western world our opportunities are great, so is the measure of our responsibilities.

In all time of our wealth,
Good Lord deliver us.

6

PROSPERITY IS GOD

WE now take a closer look at prosperity. What does it mean to be better off? It means a growing volume of goods and services available for people to use and a growing national income per head; it means better health services, more education, more entertainment and culture. Greater productivity releases effort for making other things, or for leisure and relaxation. Obviously the growing national income is an average rate of progress and the distribution of it varies. Likewise, economic progress does not mean more of everything in equal proportion. There are still some shortages and waiting lists.

There is also the Cult of Bigness. Once we reach one level of success and prosperity, there are still higher plateaux to be reached on the never-ending ascent. A noted psycho-analyst, who has spent years in both Europe and America, writes: "The analyst sees his patients—physicians, lawyers, engineers, bankers, advertising men, teachers and laboratory research men of universities, students, clerks—engaged in a marathon race, their eager faces distorted by strain, their eyes focussed not upon their goal but upon each other with a mixture of hate, envy and admiration. Panting and perspiring, they run and never arrive. They would all like to stop but dare not as long as the others are running."

Oddly enough, there is just now both in Britain and America a curious resistance to additional leisure. Since the end of the war the demand for a shorter working week has really been a demand for more overtime payment. The theoretic and contractual working week in this country has declined from 47.5 to 40 hours: the actual working week has increased from 45.4 to 47.2 hours. The latter figure may be a considerable underestimate: no allowance has been made for the fact that one worker in six now does a second job which averages 12 hours per week. The trend in America is equally interesting. Average weekly factory earnings for a $41\frac{1}{2}$ hour week are now up to a record £39 13s. In spite of what we hear about the 4-day or 20-hour week across the Atlantic, the present working week is 41.3 hours, the highest figure since the end of World War Two; average weekly overtime of 3.2 hours is the highest since the Bureau of Labour started records in 1956. Almost 4 million Americans hold two jobs ("moonlighting"). Many of them are public service employees whose working hours leave them time to take a second job. Thus the present trend seems to indicate that we are all working longer to earn more money. *Six* days shalt thou labour!

In what ways then are we better off?

WAGES

In 1964 hourly wage rates in British industry rose by 4.6 per cent, a fraction more than they did in 1963 when the increase was 4.5 per cent. During 1965 wages rose 9 per cent and the cost of living rose 4.6 per cent. Over the last 10 years, for every shilling that prices have risen, earnings have risen by 2s. 1d.; even allowing for all price increases in 1965–66. By 1957 the rise in wages was 20 per cent more than that needed to keep pace with the price index. In 1960 the figure was 32 per cent and by 1965 it had reached the record figure of 49 per cent. In the United States personal incomes rose by £35 per person in 1965. After allowing for increases in prices, the average American's purchasing power went up by $3\frac{1}{2}$ per cent.

In 1965 $10\frac{1}{2}$ million workers had pay increases averaging 9s. 9d. per week. In the past three months the index of hourly wage rates has increased 2.8 per cent while the cost of living has risen 1.8 per cent. According to the Ministry of Labour the average weekly wage for male workers in 1966 is £19 19s. 6d. (this amount—before tax—includes overtime). The average earnings for all white collar workers is now £24 2s. 2d., an increase of 4.8 per cent in 12 months. Obviously the fact that average wage rises have exceeded the average price increase by 49 per cent in the last decade indicates that we are all better off. Some wages have risen 10–20 per cent faster than prices and other wages have risen 80–100 per cent faster. The highest paid group of workers are in printing, car manufacturing, air transport, cement and oil refining (all over £22) and the lowest paid are agricultural workers, local government manual workers, operatives in made-up textile plants, boot and shoe repairers (all under £14). Full time women employees average £9 16s. 4d. for a working week of 39.1 hours, a wage increase of 51 per cent since 1956.

It is very difficult to assess the value of fringe benefits, which are almost universal but not included in the above estimates. For example, when the modest salary scales of Britain's 280,000 teachers are mentioned, it is very rare to include the generous allowances for being qualified or holding responsibility or the opportunity to earn in the holidays—these extras add hundreds of pounds to many teachers' pay and can increase the basic scale by as much as 40–50 per cent. Another example is the train driver. With the 9 per cent increase at the beginning of 1965 (6 per cent in 1964) the *minimum* rate for train drivers is £16 8s. plus any overtime : it is rarely mentioned that the driver also has free rail travel for himself and his family. Two million people travel free on British Rail in this way, while the rest of the community pay millions on expensive fares. We are not citing isolated cases—a rail guard can now earn £40–£45 a week in the most advantageous conditions. Or we could quote the clergy. Clergy pay is dropping back and back and we get no overtime and hardly any expenses of office. *But even we have our fringe benefits,* which are often not mentioned : our homes, our extra fees and offerings, our family allowances, our freedom and our security.

It is true that prices have risen steadily during 1965–66. In fact the cost of living has risen considerably more in the past two years in Britain than it has in America in the last seven years. At the end of 1965 the U.S. cost of living index is only 10.9 per cent above the figure for the 1957–59 base period. Indeed one of the truly impressive features of "the dynamic society" is that manufacturing costs have been held stable. The index of wholesale industrial prices was 101.3 in 1959 and 101.9 at the end of 1965. The index of U.S. wholesale prices is almost precisely where it stood 10 years ago, while retail prices of goods (as opposed to services) have advanced little more than 10 per cent. Hundreds of price lists and official quotations have remained unchanged for four years or longer. As prices have risen in Britain so have wages, savings and pensions. Last month, for example, pay increases were given to 2,429,000 employees. They shared an extra £906,200 a week. There were 166 stoppages last month involving 63,400 workers. These figures are from the current *Ministry of Labour Gazette*. Anyone who studies official publications will know that hundreds of thousands of British workers are receiving new wage increases every week. In 1965 productivity rose just over 1 per cent and we were demanding, and taking, wage increases of 9 per cent and profit inceases of 5 per cent. We should all heed America's example where the unions have kept their wages within their $3\frac{1}{2}$ per cent productivity increase for years—and have thus kept prices steady and wages worth every dollar.

The average British family spent a record of £20 17s. 9d. per week last year according to a Ministry of Labour survey. This figure excludes direct taxation, mortgages and savings; of these the largest are income tax and surtax, which together took £2 4s. 2d. on average. The average income of the 3400 families studied was £24 3s., an increase of 7 per cent on the previous year. The Chancellor of the Exchequer said recently that personal savings were estimated to have been 9.1, 8.0 and 8.6 per cent of personal disposal income during the past three years.

The prosperity pattern is very similar in the U.S. More and more Americans are beginning to lead a double life! It may be a second home in the country, or a boat, or some other form of escapism. For the first time rising incomes and increasing leisure are making it possible to think of holidays all the year round. This is reflected in such things as the booming sales of boats, caravans and sports goods of every description. Weekend profits from a single ski lift in America are greater than the annual profits of many Midland factories! By 1965 the holiday agreements of 53 per cent of American firms had provided for four weeks' holiday. At least one major firm (Rand Corporation of California) is actually paying its employees a substantial bonus to *make* them take a holiday. The plan is working well, but there are still a number of scientists who cannot tear themselves away. The trouble is that these boffins become so immersed in their work that they forget to take holidays!

STOCK EXCHANGE

Two out of every three people in Britain are connected in some way with the Stock Exchange, but many do not realise that their money is invested there. The Trade Union Congress is estimated to have investments of about £115 million and the Church of England is also a big investor. The present value of the capital funds held by Church Commissioners is over £300 million. And trade unions are showing undimmed enthusiasm for backing private enterprise. For years powerful unions held Socialist created gilt-edged (or government) stocks like "Daltons". Tired of seeing them go down, a number switched large sums into Ordinary shares. For example, the National Union of General and Municipal Workers, with equity holdings worth more than £1 million, has sizeable holdings in steel, property and insurance—three share groups which have been specially vulnerable to Labour policy. The National Union of Railwaymen holds shares in more than 50 companies.

There are $3\frac{1}{2}$ million small investors today and their number rises all the time. Last winter one Midland town laid on a series of lectures for small investors. The lecturer expected about 25 to enrol. When he turned up to give his first talk, he found 500 waiting to sign on. They included ex-Servicemen, farmers, housewives and small shopkeepers. How revealingly this lights up the rising living standards of the ordinary folk of Britain and their shrewd concern to make the most of their savings. Even so it is becoming fashionable at the present to switch out of shares into antiques for profitable investment. (We wonder whether the Church of England and the trade unions have enough antiques already.)

The London Stock Exchange gives employment to about 20,000 people. The aggregate value of shares of the 4500 companies quoted is £40,000 million, plus £20,000 million gilt-edged stocks. New company names added to the official quotation lists have averaged three a week during the past year. However, the rate of attrition, mostly through mergers and take-overs, but with some liquidations, has been greater and the number of companies quoted has declined slightly over the last decade.

The monthly turnover figures indicate that the total value of purchases and sales of securities of all kinds can be around a thousand million. On an average day the turnover can be £40–60 million. The average bargain in Ordinary shares is £860, mainly because of large institutional buying.

American companies are believed to have invested over £1500 million in Britain, and profits earned here by overseas companies increased by 18 per cent to £158 million. Foreign investment by British companies last year was £233 million, bringing the accumulated portfolio total to over £3800 million, plus £6000 million direct investments. Overseas profits were £312 million. Almost 60 per cent of British investment was in the sterling area, chiefly Australia, but the amount going to Europe has risen. The value of the British Government's portfolio of American bonds and industrial shares has reached £580 million; almost all the issues are "blue chips". Total British holdings in U.S. companies have doubled since 1950 to over £1000 million and Britain is by far the largest European investor in the United States. The real strain on our balances of payments account over the last eight years has come from a doubling of Government spending abroad and not from private investment, which has in fact remained static. This is not surprising: in 1965 out of every £100 profit from a direct investment in India, £80 would be absorbed in taxes in India and this country.

The Stock Market is very sensitive and it was remarkable that it lost so little ground during 1965–66. The *Financial Times* Industrial Ordinary Share Index rose 1.1 per cent whereas Wall Street had a brilliant year with the Dow Jones Industrial average up to 14.5 per cent. Perhaps the London Market is too sensitive: a company failure can rock the House. Last week record export figures were announced, plus lower imports. The market went ahead very strongly that morning; but in the afternoon a large company announced *only slightly higher* profits (£37.65 million pre-tax; £37.55 million previous year) and this disappointed the market and wiped out all gains achieved by the export figures. Invariably the Market is "tricky", because it depends on many factors, international, economic, political and domestic; there is no doubt that the Capital Gains Tax is now having a serious and crippling effect on turnover.

Misunderstandings about the Stock Exchange are widespread. It always *seems* the rich capitalists are making millions, that prices are always rising, and that profits and dividends get bigger and bigger. This is not true. Shares can go down and dividends can be reduced. The *Financial Times* Index was started 31 years ago (July 1, 1935 = 100) and has risen less than the cost of living index. The following table shows the percentage changes which have taken place in the past 12 months in some of the principal equity sections of the *Financial Times* Actuaries Share Indices:

Tobacco	+ 10.4	Steel	+ 0.9	Breweries	− 8.6
Gold Mines	+ 9.9	Oil	− 0.3	Machine Tools	− 10.9
Textiles	+ 4.1	Banks	− 1.9	Household goods	− 14.5
Newspapers	+ 0.2	Shipping	− 5.8	Stores	− 22.3
Motors	+ 1.8	Insurance	− 6.8	Property	− 26.5

It is beyond dispute that countless ordinary folk invest on Wall Street and on the London Stock Exchange. Indeed there are so many deals below £100 that commission rates have been adjusted recently to cover the costs of small deals. This morning's mail brings a typical example. Our dividend is for £1 2s. 1d. (This is a cut of 25 per cent from last year's £1 9s. 2d.: we are glad that the company's employees are not having a cut of 25 per cent in wages and salaries in order to keep pace with dividends.) Of course there are big deals—thousands of pounds—but these are usually agencies investing *our money*: *our* pension scheme, *our* unit trusts, *our* assurance premiums, *our* union subscriptions.

Wall Street is similar. The 1965–66 Census of Shareowners reckons that there are now 20 million people holding shares in public companies, treble the number of 1952. Their average household income is £3400 a year, not high by American standards and more than 3 million earn less than £1800 a year.

One of every six adults now owns shares. Professional and technical people form the biggest group of shareholders, with clerical and sales people next. The number of share-owning labourers and "operatives" has grown from 439,000 to 647,000 since 1963, the biggest percentage rise of any employed professional group.

It is also beyond dispute that folk can lose money by playing the Stock Market. We should be very thankful that wages and salaries are *not* tied to dividends and profits: otherwise thousands of workers in some companies and nationalised industries would be getting lower wages more often than not. In any case, when a company is making record profits year after year, *the whole community benefits because over 64 per cent of the distributed profits goes in taxation to the Inland Revenue.* If the 4500 companies quoted on the Stock Exchange merely "broke even" each year, it would not be *only* the shareholders who suffer. The Government would lose hundreds of millions which would have to be raised by taxation.

Let us give three examples. In the autumn of 1963 we instructed our broker to watch a particular company and buy when the market seemed right. The watching lasted over three months and the shares were bought at 16s. 1½d. on 2nd January, 1964. In that year the company announced substantially increased profits and paid a higher than forecast dividend. Net profits were up from £696,169 to £919,200. Yet the shares fell steadily throughout 1964 and stood at 12s. 3d. on December 31st. We have to sell them at 17s. 1½d. to merely "break even". If we sell this morning we lose 30 per cent of our money—in a company with record profits 25 per cent up on last year! How can we win?

The second example. We bought shares at 15s. 9d. in a company in 1961. Each year it has made increased profits. Last year pre-tax profits were up from £625,615 to £974,628 (58 per cent increase). The tax man took £493,299 (51 per cent). We have to sell our shares at 16s. 3d. to merely "break even". In four years they have *never* been high enough to give us 6d. per share (which would give us a 2 per cent profit for four years' investment in a record breaking company).

We bought shares in a third company in July 1961 at 13s.

It is a large company and well recommended for investment. Since 1961 the profits have been lower each year and the dividend unchanged for five years. The shares have not been above 8s. for the past two years and stand at 5s. 9d. this morning. We are not complaining. Our point is simply this: do the thousands of employees expect the same treatment as the shareholders? Do the unions or the Labour Government expect these workers to have no wage increase for five years so that they can keep pace with the dividends? We always enjoy discussing these matters with trade unionists and socialists!

HIRE PURCHASE

Britain's hire-purchase debt now stands at a record £1378 million—equal to £21 16s. around the neck of every man, woman and child in the country—nearly £100 owed in every home. But before the old cry goes up, "the country's going to the dogs", we would point out that our "never-never" debts are chicken-feed alongside the amounts we have tucked away in small savings. We have £8400 million in the National Savings, £5375 million in building societies (5 million shareholders), and £610 million in unit trusts. That little lot adds up to £261 10s. for everyone in Britain. It is true that 1965 was a gloomy year in the stock market and that there was a slower rate of growth in National Savings and in unit trusts. But even in unit trusts, for example, an *extra* £61.5 million has been tucked away in the past six months. In spite of all the talk about money being "tight" and the credit squeeze in 1965–66, a record £419 million was received by British building societies in the last 3 months, and in the past 12 months an *extra* £83 million has been put into National Savings.

We find it difficult to understand why so many families buy goods on the "never-never" instead of drawing out some of their savings to pay cash. Perhaps they do not realise that when a car is bought on the "never-never" the H.P. charges are equivalent to paying interest of at least 15 per cent a year. On furniture it can equal 25 per cent. It seems false economy to pay out such interest rates rather than use savings which are earning less than 5 per cent net.

We have now reached the ultimate in hire-purchase. We can now "buy" money on the "never-never". A new personal credit scheme now covers the country in which customers can hire-purchase "paybonds" and go shopping with them instead of banknotes or a cheque book. Customers can start off with a minimum of £25 in £5 units, and go up to £250, and with these go round nominated shops on a spending spree for anything from furs to bicycles. This seems to us to be putting an irresistible new temptation to overspend into a shopper's hands. In a later section we shall point out that worrying over too much H.P. is *one* factor among many which contributes to mental illness.

GAMBLING

Last year people in the United Kingdom spent more money on gambling activities than in any previous year. The overall turnover for all forms of gambling increased to £930 million. Broken down into simple figures, if this sum were distributed back to the public, every man, woman and child in Britain could expect to receive nearly £17 or about 6s. 6d. every week for 52 weeks.

Betting on greyhound racing was £110 million, on football pools £73 million, on horse racing £615 million, on fixed odds football £65 million and on bingo £35 million. There are now 15,500 betting shops and this number is increasing rapidly and it is estimated that over 12 million people do the pools every week. It is not generally realised that no football pool returns more than 7s. 11d. in dividends for every £1 staked. One returns only 6s. 8d. and the average return is 7s. 7d. Of the £73 million staked last year, £24 million went in taxation—from 1965 the tax payable is 25 per cent instead of 33 per cent. We would say that pools winners are virtually "taxed" already without incorporation in any capital gains tax, because a third of the stakes sent in by the public is now absorbed in running expenses and 25 per cent goes in Government tax.

It is difficult to assess the extent of the bingo craze. There are 12,363 club premises: 1007 of these clubs have memberships of over 2000. The latest total of bingo club membership is put at 14,324,081. It may be that this figure is inflated because folk join more than one club—when away on holiday for example. The charges for taking part in bingo amount to about £11.7 million, and this figure does not include membership fees or stake money.

Recently there have been reports in the national press of happenings behind the gay façades of many bingo palaces which has turned them into real gambling dens. Games based on roulette have been introduced and there is a danger that it will bring untold misery into the homes of people who become addicted to it. Roulette fever seems to be afflicting women rather than men. Investigations have uncovered some heart-breaking stories of wives and mothers who pawn rings, sell clothing, go in fear of their families finding out; of women who lose £10–15 a night. It is alleged that there are thousands of husbands in Britain who would be shocked if they really knew what happened on "bingo night".

Gamblers' Anonymous does not cater for wives and mothers who are crazed with bingo or roulette, but it is trying to help poker players, horse or dog backers, or chemin-de-fer all-nighters who want to cure their compulsions. There seems to be no difference at all between the British gambling scene and the American one. There are millions of gamblers on both sides of the Atlantic and about half are estimated to be compulsive. If this is right, the amount of compulsion is formidable, for the Churches' Council on Gambling estimates that about 25 per cent of the adult population gambles regularly and seriously. Gamblers who want to try to find a cure can phone a London number for details of regular meetings to discuss their problems. There are also meetings for wives who are troubled by their husbands' gambling habits.

We have made this survey in some detail. It is essential to establish beyond doubt that there is vast spending power on both sides of the Atlantic. Money is in enormous circulation today and ordinary folks are using it and saving it. We are forced to the conclusion that our society must be described in terms of prosperity rather than poverty. Who would deny that the Western world is affluent and becoming more so? We are *not*

F

trying to prove that every family in the land is caught up in unit trusts, bingo, hire-purchase or the Stock Exchange. We would maintain, however, that ordinary homes are participating in these activities to an unsuspected degree and that collectively the *trend* is towards a financial prosperity which is increasing and very widespread.

The facts and figures of our survey indicate some of the signs of the times, and our New Testament enquiries will not be signposts for Christ's followers if we look at the affluent society "through a glass darkly". We must look face to face. We are confronted with a variety of contemporary evidence in support of our financial well-being. But money is not the only thing. There are plenty of wealthy people in our mental institutions.

We must continue to probe. The people of God cannot be Christ's "signs" in the world today until we know what is going on in society around us. We are not persuaded that Church officers and congregations are engaging the world outside in dialogue. Not many individual Christians can assess the problems of prosperity and not many congregations are aware of the challenge of affluence. How does God penetrate the affluent society? Through us?

We doubt if Christians have anything meaningful to say in society unless we continue to discover what is going on all around us. Then we shall rediscover something else, namely the supreme relevance of the New Testament to the sixties and seventies.

We have the money. What else?

BETTER HOMES

More than 25 million cookers, immersion and space heaters, refrigerators and washing-machines have been installed in Britain's homes in the past eight years. There are over 13 million combined television and sound licences and a further 3 million sound-only licences. Today 36.2 per cent of all homes have electric cookers, against 24.5 per cent a decade ago—550,000 new electric cookers being delivered in 1965. Immersion heaters have risen over the same period from 16.4 per cent to 38.9 per cent, washing-machines from 17.5 to 59.1 per cent and refrigerators from 8.1 to 41 per cent. Space heating (excluding storage heaters) has risen rather slowly, from 60.5 to 69 per cent and central heating from 2.7 to 12 per cent. Thus in a very few years washing-machines and television ownership has more than doubled and ownership of refrigerators and centrally-heated homes has increased fourfold. Turnover in the domestic appliance industry is now running at over £400 million a year. Indeed dealers and consumers alike are becoming a little bemused by the choices and various characteristics of 133 different models or sizes of cooker, 160 refrigerators, 125 washing-machines and 190 heating appliances.

Although our home comforts are increasing rapidly, our safety record is still appalling. Figures from the Royal Society for the Prevention of Accidents show that every year more than 9000 people die as a result of accidents in the home; a further 100,000 are seriously injured and 1,500,000 slightly hurt. So we still have a better chance of being killed or injured in the comfort of our own homes than on the roads!

It is worth noting that our new domestic appliances are already *out of date before we buy them.* That very latest washing-machine we have on order for 1966–67 is already replaced by a better model for 1968 now on the drawing board. The 1966 car is already a back number and this is probably now true of the 1967 models which are already "dated" at blue-print stage. By 1965 Americans had begun to change their cars every three years on average. There is status involved in all this. Take T.V. sets, for example. In Britain they are built to last 10 years on average: ours "pooped out" this week after doing continuous duty since 1952. If we have a 17-inch screen which is working satisfactorily, why should it bother us in the very least if the rest of the street have 27-inch screens? What does bother us is when they pay 8s. to 10s. rental every week quite happily and expect God to understand that they cannot commit themselves to sign a pledge card and cannot afford more than a shilling or so a week for Him.

HOLIDAYS

In 1965 over 700,000 American visitors came to Britain and some 152,000 Britons visited the States. American expenditure, including fares paid by them to British carriers, amounted to almost £100 million. Tourism is our biggest single earner of dollars. More than 2,280,000 Americans, a record, travelled abroad in 1965 and spent more money than ever before. The chief factor seems to be America's continuing prosperity. Summer in Europe is becoming the traditional graduation present. Last year travelling Americans spent some £570 million abroad. This was nearly half the country's international payments deficit (£1250 million in 1965). The American Government is taking steps, if not to discourage travel abroad, at least to make travel at home more appealing.

Over 5 million have taken their holidays abroad in 1965. Travel agents estimated that by January 1st some 3.5 million had already booked summer holidays at home and overseas. This represents a 10 per cent increase on the same period last year. In 1964 4½ million of our countrymen took their vacations abroad (25 per cent for the first time) and it cost them £225 million. It is to be hoped that they were of a kind to enhance the national reputation in the eyes of a critical Continent—for 84 per cent of them travelled in Europe. Though a third of them were motorists, the representation is no longer predominantly of the rich : indeed a fifth of them came from households with a family income of less than £950.

Tourism, personal or "packaged", is big business in both directions. It is Britain's fourth-largest export industry, earning more than £300 million a year, while over £240 million goes into foreign pockets to pay for our own holidays. It is a competitive business : the consumer gets more for his money every year. Less and less is travel rationed by the purse ; thanks to longer holidays in industry and to conveniently-planned tours, it is less and less limited by time. What may, however, threaten our enjoyment of this increasing freedom is the swamping of transport and hotel facilities.

Nearly a quarter of the Britons who went abroad in 1965 had another holiday. We are becoming a nation of two-holiday families. Last year nearly 6 million people took two holidays away from home and this figure is bound to increase. The Smiths, the Browns and the Joneses plan to go farther afield and spend more than ever before. They are paying from £17 to £150 for 15 days. In 1965 it is calculated that they spent on average £65 each on fares, hotels and pocket money. Travel agents everywhere report that there is a "mass market now" for £150 holidays. It is interesting that the majority of Britons buy our cars and washing-machines on H.P. but we prefer to pay cash for our holidays. The H.P. holiday has not caught on. The rare Briton today is the one who has *not* been abroad. And we spend around £70 million on our holiday photographs!

LONG LIVES AND EARLY MARRIAGES

Trends towards longevity and early marriages are revealed in the latest tables from the Registrar-General. Of a total population in England and Wales of 46.1 million, nearly 6 million are aged over 65 compared with under 3 million 30 years ago. Four out of every 100 teenagers between 15 and 19 are now married. The expectation of life of a boy at birth is now 68 years and of a girl 74. This is a slight fall on the previous year as a result of the higher death rates in the severe winter of 1963.

The number of retirement pensioners is rising rapidly and this will continue until about 1980 when it will slow down until it reaches about 8.5 million—nearly 40 per cent above the 1965 total. The rising cost of retirement pensions is not only due to the increases in the weekly rates of benefits but also to the rapid growth in the number of pensioners. This is presenting social and economic problems, which we shall discuss later. In 1946 there were six workers to every pensioner; in 1961 it was four workers to one pensioner. Very soon it will be three to one. In 1965 one person in nine was over 65 : by 1975 this figure will be one in every seven.

HOW PEOPLE DIE IN BRITAIN

(These figures are for 1963, the latest year for which death statistics are complete.)

Deaths from natural causes	626,045
Violent deaths	28,243
Total	654,288

The 20 Main Causes of Death

1.	Heart diseases	187,190
2.	Cancer (Lung cancer : 27,620)	116,489
3.	Blood clots	92,492
4.	Pneumonia	39,788
5.	Bronchitis	39,141
6.	Circulatory diseases (other than heart)	27,723
7.	Respiratory diseases (other than bronchitis and pneumonia)	13,628
8.	Disease of early infancy	11,119
9.	Accidents in the home	9,235
10.	Senility	7,435
11.	ROAD ACCIDENTS	6,922
12.	Suicide	6,247
13.	Congenital malformations	6,246
14.	Ulcers	4,957
15.	Accidents other than road and home	4,498
16.	Diabetes	4,470
17.	Influenza	3,647
18.	Kidney disorders	3,643
19.	T.B.	3,469
20.	Leukaemia	3,180

Some Other Causes

Arthritis	1,615	Warfare : Army	16	
Mental disorders	1,328	Navy	2	
Venereal disease	868	R.A.F.	8	26
Childbirth	296	Air accidents		25
Railway accidents	288	Lightning		6
Murder	153	Executions		2
Manslaughter	135	Motor racing		1

OUR HEALTH

Socialised medicine at last! In 1965 the Federal Government approved the health care programme, known as "medicare". £2700 million is being spent during 1966 and this will provide compulsory hospital and medical care assistance to 19 million aged Americans. Everyone over 65 is included in the scheme and the main benefit is up to 60 days of hospital bed charges and 20 days of home care for each illness. A voluntary additional guinea a month contribution will cover most of the doctors' bills. The American Medical Association fought the "medicare" proposal for more than 10 years, using ingenuity and lavish funds in advertising, lobbying and trying to influence election results. Brand a Bill "socialistic" and it stands a good chance of being thrown out! However, this bill has removed one of the great scandals of American society, the oppressive poverty of the old induced by their colossal medical bills. For this achievement great credit must be given to President Johnson.

The gross cost of the National Health Service in England and Wales in 1965 (including welfare services and welfare foods) is £1196 million. This is equivalent to £25 a head of the population. This cost represents 4.8 per cent of the national income. Abolition of prescription charges added another £50 million to the national bill (we average 6.7 prescriptions p.a.!). How is this spent? What do we get for our money? In Britain the average person went into hospital once in 14 years, but saw his general practitioner about five times a year.

In some respects the pattern which emerges is surprising. Mental disorders account for the largest expenditure, over £140 million, followed by dental treatment, chest and heart diseases and maternity services—about £50 for each baby born. Surprisingly, the treatment of cancer costs less than £24 million a year. The bulk of expenditure (56 per cent) goes on hospitals. The family doctor service costs £80 million and local health authority services cost £90 million.

There is steady expansion in hospital building. The value of building completed and in progress during 1964 rose to £386 million from £322 million in 1963. There is some informed criticism of the cost of the Health Service, for example from the Office of Health Economics, and we believe that there is some justification for criticising the extravagance of some schemes of some regional boards. In one psychiatric hospital in this Midland town two wards are being modernised at the moment. The cost? £112,000. We should have preferred £12,000 to be spent on ward improvements and £100,000 towards research into mental disorder or staff salaries. Then our priorities would be right.

Great is the temptation to believe that our National Health Service is "free". In fact it is an expensive service as any employer knows to his cost. A man earning £20 a week, with a wife and two children, pays something like £1 a week towards the National Health Service. The weekly cost per in-patient in 1965 in the general hospitals of this town average £41 13s. 5d., compared with an average cost per case of £65 18s. 8d. The weekly cost per in-patient in our particular psychiatric hospital is £13 14s. 1d.

Our medical care is excellent, but there are serious problems. We are worried about staff shortages and poor pay. Doctors are emigrating at a steady rate of 900 a year and doctors from overseas fill 40 per cent of the junior hospital posts. Nurses are emigrating at a rate of 2500 a year and most hospitals would close if they had no coloured nurses. There are more than 170,000 full-time nurses and midwives and 60,000 part-time in N.H.S. hospitals, and 23,000 doctors in general practice. But nursing pay and conditions are inadequate, and many qualified nurses and hospital technicians work freelance through agencies at two and three times their former income. Some hospitals have to rely on the agencies for 30–40 per cent of their nurses. This is one of several examples of inadequate pay costing the N.H.S. dearly.

Illness cost Britain over 300 million working days in 1965. This figure is the same as in immediate previous years—compared with an average 2–3 million working days lost in strikes. Each insured person had an average of 14 days off work during the year. Married women have an average just over three weeks' sickness absence a year, almost a week more than single women. More than £180 million was paid in sickness benefits, equivalent to about one-sixth of the total expenditure of the National Health Service: this generosity is increasing absenteeism!

SOCIAL SECURITY

Prosperity is not for the rich alone, nor is it confined to a tiny minority. This is one of the good things about taxation. Families on low incomes pay no income tax, no school fees, no medical bills and generally live in a subsidised council house. The *top* rent on this estate, for example, is 49s. for a modern three-bedroom house with two toilets (and no rates of course): and with a garage! In some parts of England councils are beginning to build two-garage houses.

The total effect of taxation brings about a much greater equality and social security than there seems to be if we look only at the range of incomes as they are received. The amounts received are very unequal; the amounts retained, after taxes have been paid, are much less unequal. If, in addition to this, we take into account the effects of income derived from the Welfare State, whether in the form of direct money grants or in the value of food subsidies and social services, the movement towards greater equality is very strong.

We must pause to examine taxation for a moment. Have most of us any idea how much we *really* pay in tax each year? If we were asked to guess would we be within £10, or even £100 of the true amount to be extracted from us in 1966–67? Most of us soon work out how much we pay the Exchequer at 3s. 3d. tax on every gallon of petrol, plus of course the £17 10s. road licence. And most of us soon studied the tax tables in the newspapers to find how much extra will be taken in P.A.Y.E. We ourselves could not do this: all the papers we looked in to find how much extra for a married man with two children *started with incomes £4 per week more than we earn!* It would be tedious to reproduce our tax tables and statistics, but P.A.Y.E. and petrol duty is only about half of what most of us pay in taxation. Have we forgotten purchase tax, rates, national insurance? On close examination the £2500-a-year man, with a car, a wife and two children, with average-moderate tastes, *loses £20 a week—£2* out of every £5 he earns—to keep the Welfare State going.

Indeed, Britain's high rate of taxation is one probable reason for our ailing economy. A heavy income tax burden is a disincentive to production. In America a man with a wife and two children earning £3570 a year pays £397 in Federal income tax compared with £765 in income tax in Britain. A man with a wife and two children earning £1750 p.a. pays £103 in American Federal tax and £275 in British tax.

In America, too, low-income families are eligible for rent subsidies as a result of the Omnibus Housing Bill. Its rent subsidy provision, costing £124 million will make 375,000 apartment units available for needy families during 1966–67. A family qualifying for the subsidy has to pay 25 per cent of its income towards an economic rent based on the housing cost to the builder. Grants up to £550 are offered to low-income families wanting to improve their homes.

There are very few working homes today where the *only* income is the wage packet and comparatively few pensioners have *only* the state pension to support them. By the end of 1965 the cost of all payments being made by the Ministry of Pensions and National Insurance was at a rate of £1790 million. The average number of people who pay weekly contributions is 24.8 million and about 13 million pay graduated pension contributions. All members of the community are rightly benefiting from social security. Indeed the National Assistance Board is having to step up its anti-fraud campaign. It now has 96 trained detectives throughout Britain carrying out major investigations. About 40 people are prosecuted each week. In any one week the number of benefits and allowances being paid is now 13 million. Family allowances are being paid to nearly 4 million families containing over 9.5 million children. We wonder how family allowances are actually spent and whether they are still universally necessary. In any case, of our own weekly family allowance, for example, 3s. 2d. goes straight back to another Government department in income tax, thus helping to maintain full employment. Last year a weekly average of 975,000 claimed sickness benefit and 363,000 claimed unemployment benefit (unfilled vacancies averaged 320,000 each week). The number of retirement pensions has risen to over 6 million, and about 625,000 war pensions are being paid, including 473,000 disablement pensions and 130,000 widows pensions.

Recent changes in American tax structures are of great significance. Many taxes are being *lowered* : this is contributing to an expanding economy, lower prices, less unemployment and a stable cost of living. The tax cuts are in several phases, and there is an immediate cut of £621 million in 1966, including reductions in the tax on cars worth £200 million. Another £170 million is being cut each year until 1969. The tax cut that almost every American appreciates is the reduction from 10 per cent to 5 per cent in the tax on new cars. On average this reduces the price of a new car by about £45. Retail taxes have been *removed entirely* from radios, televisions, cameras, refrigerators, records and record players, jewellery, luggage and toilet articles, car spares, musical instruments and most electrical appliances. Taxes on entertainment and telephones are also being abolished. The President announced that these cuts were possible because the flourishing state of the economy is increasing the yields from all sources of tax. Even the heavy burden of defence spending is being off-set by the expansion throughout the nation. And there is no sign of the American economy "levelling off".

All these figures and benefits indicate that social security is enjoyed widely in every community in America and Britain. This is a good thing and is doing much to eliminate hardship and worry. *It does not relieve greed and envy. We feel that these are increasing.*

> *From envy, hatred and malice and all uncharitableness,*
> *Good Lord, deliver us.*

EDUCATION

Educational expenditure by public authorities in Britain, including school meals and milk, has more than trebled in 12 years, reaching £1617 million in 1965–66. This represents 5.5 per cent of the gross national product, compared with 3.4 per cent twelve years ago. Meals and milk cost taxpayers £67.4 million.

Our school population is nearly 8 million aged between 2 and 19. If the number of live births rises to a million in the eighties, as is forecast, then the school population will be around 11.5 million in 20 years hence. About half a million boys and girls attend our 7250 independent schools. Lord Shawcross said "I do not know a single member of the Labour Party, who can afford to do so, who does not send his children to a public school, often at great sacrifice—not for snobbish reasons or to perpetuate class distinction, but to ensure his children get the best".

The proportion of children benefiting from higher education is increasing. Ten years ago only 7.8 per cent of the 17-year-olds in the country were remaining at school voluntarily, while in 1966 some 14 per cent are doing so. Allowing for increases in the size of age groups there was a rise of 42 per cent in eight years in the number of school-leavers with five or more "O" level passes in the General Certificate of Education. One school-leaver in every six has five "O" levels and one in every 13 has two or more "A" level passes. About one school-leaver in every seven goes on to further full-time education at universities, colleges of advanced technology and teacher training colleges. There are 333,000 teachers in grant-aided schools and 280,000 in maintained primary and secondary schools. Less than one teacher in four is a graduate and we hope that this proportion will rise with the general level of education.

In 1970–71 the statutory school-leaving age will be raised from 15 to 16. This means that pupils whose 16th birthdays fall on or after 2nd September 1971, must stay at school until Easter of the following year at least. Taking this into account, the statisticians estimate that in 20 years' time over a quarter of all 17-year-olds and 10 per cent of all 18-year-olds will still be at school.

Our widespread system of "free" education is a true blessing, giving every child the opportunity to develop talents and ability and thus go on to a worthwhile and creative job in the community. But there are big problems. It is said that there are grave shortages of teachers. (We wonder about this: a close friend of ours who is a well-qualified graduate with 12 years' teaching experience, tried for a move last year. He applied for over 60 advertised posts, and sent full particulars, but only four called him for interview.) Certainly a more serious difficulty is major building deficiency in a large number of schools. Here are details of four selected deficiencies which infringe the express provisions of the school building regulations, and the number of pupils affected by them.

Major deficiencies in schools

Specified Features	Schools Primary	Schools Secondary	Schools All	Pupils (1000s) Primary	Pupils (1000s) Secondary	Pupils (1000s) All
No warm water supply for pupils	6101	373	6474	682.4	142.1	824.5
No kitchen or scullery on site	4647	491	5138	674.7	170.6	845.3
No staff room	8750	95	8845	766.3	26.7	793.0
Seriously substandard site	9211	1553	10,764	1414.6	631.7	2046.3

An estimated £1568 million is required at present costs to bring all primary and secondary schools up to date and to raise the leaving age to 16. Surely in 1965 there need not be 202 schools without electricity? But again we must note that this is not a local British problem. The belief that American school buildings are more modern and better equipped than those in Britain is contradicted by a survey carried out by the U.S. Department of Health, Education and Welfare. It shows that in several respects conditions are worse than in British schools. Of the 48 million American pupils enrolled in 1965, nearly 8 million attended schools regarded as fire hazards. While in Britain only one in 850 attend schools with no piped water, in America the figure is one in 280.

The number of schoolgirl mothers is steadily increasing. The proportion of 15-year-old girls who have illegitimate babies is now one schoolgirl in 350. This represents 6 per cent of all illegitimate births. It is difficult to get accurate figures about venereal diseases among young people of school age, but they are definitely alarming and on the increase. Fat children are becoming a worry too! Their number is increasing. About one child in every 30 is seriously overweight, and the American figure may be one in 10. Experts say that fatness is now the most frequent nutritional disturbance in a wealthy country. Most overweight children grow into overweight adults and serious effects can follow.

Another problem, which is certainly Transatlantic, is that with the widespread increase in higher education, it is tempting to assume that all children are capable of using this opportunity. Of course every child with the ability should go on to college and university, and this is becoming increasingly possible. To maintain that every child should *not* go on to higher education is not to deny freedom or rights; it is to recognise that although all children should have equal chances, some are cleverer than others. American parents are being warned not to "wheedle" their children into going to university. Hundreds of young men and women who were urged against their will to attend college, are dropping out before completing their courses. Pennsylvania State University prepared a report last year showing that a

national average of 45 per cent of all university students leave
before graduation. Yale has a "drop-out" average of one in four
and Princeton one in five.

During the academic year 1966–67 some 4000 students will
leave British universities without a degree. It is as if two complete universities the size of Sheffield and Keele were wiped out.
The financial cost has been estimated at £5 million every year.
The human cost is beyond measurement. The "wastage" rate
for all British Universities is 14 per cent. Four out of five of these
fail for academic reasons; the rest because of personal problems,
and hardly any for disciplinary troubles.

It is an expensive business for the nation to provide "free"
education for our children. There is not much left out of
£10,000 when a child is educated from 5 until 21. Those who
benefit from school, college and university training are in great
debt to the rest of the community. We feel that there might be
less agitation for increased salaries in the professions today if
more of us would recognise our debt to the taxpayer for finan-
cing an education which has probably lasted for 15–16 years.
Most of us would be nothing without education and most of us
had it subsidised if not virtually free.

Only a fool or rank amateur would attempt to survey
America's schools in similar detail. Anything we might say about
them in general can be proven wrong by the citation of a
perfectly good particular case somewhere. This very fact is often
offered as proof of the system's strength—its diversity—and as
equally convincing proof of its weakness—its chaos. In the
current year some 48 million pupils are enrolled in all types of
schools—public, private and church—from kindergarten to high
school. University remains American education's most basic goal
and the proportion of teenagers going on to higher education is
truly impressive. The public schools are the American equivalent
of Britain's county council schools. They are publicly financed
and controlled by local school boards, under the supervision of
the education authorities, of each of the 50 states; and they
account for the overwhelming majority of the total pupils. The
largest non-public sector is that of the Roman Catholic parochial
schools, housing close to 6 million youngsters. This leaves only a

small fraction of education to the private schools and there are probably no more than 350,000 places in the equivalents of the British public schools. For higher education there are 2139 colleges and universities in all parts of the States. Although some of their course offerings would be reckoned below university level in Britain, 455 of the institutions offer work up to the master's degree and 223 grant the doctorate.

Thus in the United States, as in Britain, a vast continuing expansion in education is under way. Whatever may be said of comparative Anglo-American standards of quality, none can gainsay the massive quantitative advantage which the American people enjoy: last year they had a school enrolment of 92 per cent of the population aged 14 to 17, and a college or university enrolment of 39 per cent of all persons between 18 and 21. If knowledge and its dissemination are the key to progress, America and Britain are striving hard to achieve both.

WORTH NOTING

Perhaps some Britons have not heard of muscular atrophy. It is seriously maintained that Americans, who have very largely lost the use of their legs because of dependence on the cars which symbolise their mobility, are now in danger of losing the use of their hands as a result of the growing popularity of battery-operated gadgets. The electric razor, the electric typewriter and the family dishwashing machine paved the way, but now there are more and more implements, many of which do not need to be plugged into an electric socket.

Among the gadgets advertised in America in 1966 are a shoe-cleaning kit and an electric knife which takes all the work out of carving roast beef and turkey. Even the effort of cleaning teeth has now been eliminated with battery-operated brushes and battery-operated wristwatches are getting rid of the old-fashioned chore of winding. We particularly enjoy the gadget which opens garage doors automatically without our leaving the car, and the water which flows automatically when a glass is held under the tap. Happily the increasing use of computers and adding machines makes it unnecessary to think about the probable ultimate outcome. You can cook by remote control!

We are trying to give a wide and varied survey of social conditions and economic activity in order to share our conviction that prosperity is spreading far and wide. Here are a few further angles on our lives, stated briefly to supplement previous information and to narrow the possibility that we are being selective in our presentation.

1. One in every four families now live in a subsidised council house and 47 per cent own their own homes (28 per cent in 1951). Some councils are now having to lift the income limit from £20 per week to £25, otherwise they would not be able to find sufficient families to qualify. Exchequer subsidies for council houses in Britain totalled £88 million in 1965.

2. Three-quarters of the men and half the women in Britain smoke cigarettes. Men smoke on average 19 a day and women 11 : a lot of money going up in smoke! Britain's smoking bill last year was £1330 million of which about £1000 million went to the Government as tax.

Americans smoked an estimated 533,000 million cigarettes during the past 12 months, despite the publicity linking smoking with cancer. This record figure is 8000 million higher than 1964. In New York State each packet sold must bear a label with this message: "Warning. Excessive use is dangerous to health".

3. Brewers have just had their best year since 1947, producing 29.5 million barrels, and Britons "downed" 1032 million gallons. This represents nine glasses a week for every man, woman and child.

4. Television is in 15 million homes—86 per cent of all private households—and its grip on our national life, its influence on our habits and way of life are perceptibly increasing. According to the latest Post Office figures there are about 2 million homes with television sets but no licences. New sets delivered to retailers last year numbered 1.9 million. It was a little short of miraculous that over *350 million people* watched Sir Winston Churchill's funeral "live". Folk living till 75 spend an average of $12\frac{1}{2}$ years watching T.V.

5. The increasing problem of abandoned cars is worrying many local authorities, particularly in London. More than 6000 cars were left abandoned in London streets last year. In Birmingham an average of 200 transistor radio sets are thrown away in the streets each week. And in America the "town dump" is an increasing landscape feature.

6. British women spend something like £100 million a year on cosmetics and toiletries. Hair preparations pull in another £40 million and an additional £70 million goes into the hairdressers' till for service and skill. The cost of joining the face race in America is equally staggering and leads the market with £230 million on hair preparations, with an extra £35 million on hair colouring. Skin-care preparations are a £50 million market in the States, and make-up sales are running close to £180 million.

We have tried to probe into prosperity in some detail. Ideally we should each make our own diagnosis of our times and circumstances, a point we made earlier. "Go ye into all the world" means nothing unless it means being involved in the nineteen-sixties and being aware of what is going on. The Western world is a world of progress and prosperity, and people are coming from other parts to live here and share our good fortune. We do not always realise that we are the envy of many. By the grace of God we have been born into a land of plenty and not into India or Africa.

Prosperity has its problems. Indeed it is possible to make a strong case against the affluent society because it has brought so many vexing issues before us. We can say this without minimising the great and widespread benefits of prosperity. But if we say that we have no problems we deceive ourselves and the truth is not in us. Affluence and Christian responsibility present problems for the one, possibilities for the other. We cannot contract out. We are citizens and a good Christian must be a good citizen. As such we are forced to recognise the signs of the times. Remedies can be found. In every problem of prosperity there is need of Christ.

7

UP GO THE COSTS

What are the things which are flourishing in the midst of prosperity? Can folk on either side of the Atlantic deny that what are flourishing and growing today are crime, venereal disease, suicide, bankruptcy, juvenile delinquency, drug addiction, mental disorders, strikes, bad debts.

. . . What are the symptoms? . . . are they not common to each one of us? . . . speed, noise and strain of modern life . . . pressures of group behaviour . . . too much money and too much leisure . . . materialism and general lack of consideration . . . problems and opportunities for young people . . . world insecurity and consequent escapism . . . relaxation of moral standards and of public opinion . . . irrelevance and triviality of much Church life.

It is difficult to separate problems from prosperity. Both are part of the twentieth century. We each feel strongly that we have more problems and less prosperity than other people, but all this does is to make us more discontented in the midst of affluence. We ourselves have been in refugee camps in the Middle East and also lived and worked among survivors from Nazi concentration camps: we know that in the West we have prosperity in the midst of the most pressing problems. Even in our discussion so far, problems have been peeping through our survey of prosperity. H.P. is a problem . . . immigration is a problem . . . sex is a problem . . . school-building is a problem. Of these and many other important aspects of community and individual life it is evident that there is good and bad in them. We are not convinced that there is any aspect of affluence which is clearly an unqualified blessing. In this discussion we are bound to group our findings into some sequence, but this is not because we believe that we can divide the signs of the times into neat compartments labelled "prosperity" and "hardship". Indeed it would seem to be equally permissible to discuss hire-purchase, new cars, gambling, or status under the problems of the day as it is to include them in any consideration of our abundant welfare. Or in which category do we put living under a pay pause or under a Government which cannot prevent a rapid rise in costs and prices? This is personal choice, and will depend partially on our presuppositions and "blinkers". We noted earlier that the accuracy and relevance of this discussion depends on it being appreciated more in terms of a spiral than a straight line or neat pattern.

We must continue our probe. We shall examine some of the major features of Western civilisation which ought to be vexing all Christians. Certainly we have seen these aspects of affluence in every type of community on both sides of the Atlantic. The more prosperous we become, the more these problems nag and oppress us. At first sight they might appear to be neither serious nor widespread : however a penetrating look at our own local communities will help us not to underestimate these signs of the times and the need of Christ in the midst. We can easily discover for ourselves whether we live in an age of anxiety and aspirins, of vice and venereal disease, of suicide and selfishness, of dis-ease and doubt.

MENTAL ILLNESS

Africa is our best starting place. Mental diseases are widespread and increasing on that continent but their treatment is receiving little priority. The happy African savage lying in the sun without any worries is a myth. The drift from villages to towns, taking jobs in industry and migration from area to area in search of jobs is leading to considerable increase in mental disturbances, especially among young people. With 40 per cent of Africa's young under the age of 15, the crime rate, juvenile delinquency, prostitution, alcoholism, illegitimacy, drug abuse and suicide are all going up, leading to many mental cripples. Recent tribal clashes have also been traced to mental disorders. Epidemic outbreaks of laughing attacks, not unlike the mass hysteria associated with the Beatles, have recently occurred among 11–14-year-olds. The social ills are seldom noticed by visitors; just as in Europe and America the mentally ill are hidden from public view.

Yes, Africa was a strange starting point for mental illness. It is sobering to realise that this is part of the Western influence too. We know all too little about mental illnesses. How many people realise that in our hospitals at any one time we are caring for some 200,000 mentally disordered patients—that is, about half the country's total hospital population? Treatment is costing the country well over £140 million every year (and this does not include thousands of the working days lost by patients who are physically fit but cannot work). This is Britain's most costly disorder, almost twice as expensive as any other single group of diseases. Most of this money is spent on hospital treatment. Mental hospitals spend only about a quarter of the amount devoted by general hospitals to food and other necessities for their patients. In our own hospital we spend £1 19s. 9d. on feeding a patient for a week, of which 11s. 7d. goes on salaries and wages. Another example of austerity is that a mental hospital must have an average of at least 750 patients of one denomination before that denomination can have a full-time chaplain. With the rapid turnover of patients who stay less than three months, the total number of different patients must thus be some 1200–1500 before a full-time appointment is permitted and in addition a chaplain is expected to minister to the hundreds of staff. This means that time for specialised pastoral counselling and staff consultation is severely curtailed by the Ministry of Health regulations. If mental hospitals were allowed to provide more adequately, the cost of treatment could easily be double what it is.

A quarter of Britain's adults are socially handicapped by psychiatric symptoms, according to research by the Mental Health Research Fund. About 100,000 people in Britain are thought to suffer in some degree from an anxiety neurosis called agoraphobia. This is a dread of public places, even a terror of going out of doors: fear holds them prisoner in their own homes. Probably about one person in 12 is suffering from fairly severe neurotic disorder. This means about one family in every three or four is likely to have a member who is mentally ill. The teenagers' "worry clinics" which began in London in 1961 are flooded with youngsters. The number of neurotics seen by

*Britain's 23,000 family doctors has shown an alarming increase
in the past five years. An anonymous doctor has quoted busy
G.P.s as saying that half of their patients "seem to be going
bonkers". As to the reason for the increase in neurotics, "Many
of us have an uneasy feeling that the Welfare State is making us
into a nation of softies".*

Family doctors care for over 400,000 mentally disabled
patients a year. This figure will probably increase because tran-
quillisers and other drugs are considerably reducing the number
of patients in mental hospitals. The latest figures (1965) available
from the Office of Health Economics show that in that year
32.1 million working days were lost through mental disorders
and a further 4 million from depression and nervousness. The
community has not derived any benefits in reduction of sickness
absence through the changing patterns and improvements of
medical care. One accident in every 3 is caused by "tension".

Mental difficulties can begin at an early age. It can start with
loneliness and insecurity before the age of 5. Most children
worry to some extent about school, most take time to adapt
themselves to an unfamiliar place. It is said that girls are more
introverted than boys and tend to hug and prolong their fears.
Children's worries about school fall into two main categories:
those relating to work and those concerning their relationships
with one another. Unfortunately many of these young worriers
are those who, because of their reticence, are most likely to be
overlooked by their teachers. If children are worrying per-
sistently about work, then to some extent surely the school is to
blame. Then young worriers grow into tense teenagers. . . .

This picture of mental disturbance is duplicated in most
Western countries, including the United States. Ten years ago
New York Juvenile authorities predicted that 33 of a selected
group of 301 6-year-old boys would fall into delinquency before
they were much older. The authorities said at the same time
that 243 boys would keep out of trouble. All but 13 were true
to the prediction. The remaining 25 were given an even chance
and nine became delinquent. Disorder and delinquency can
often be diagnosed and treated successfully at an early stage. We
are not sure whether there is in fact much more mental sickness

today, but certainly there is more awareness and recognition these days, and more time to be ill. Years ago folk could not afford to take a few weeks off work or from looking after a family in order to be mentally ill.

Who are those who suffer in this way? Numbers, daunting as they are, give little clue to people. The gravity of mental illness lies in its infinite complex nature, which more than any other affliction tends to involve the whole of the patient's personality. The risks of affliction appear increasingly to stem from the tensions and stresses of modern society. Who are these "victims" of prosperity? They come from every age and background. We cannot go into details but we ourselves are perplexed because our patients are so different. Wealthy men, pretty teenagers, students, beautiful women, men with important jobs—the folks of "Park Lane" as well as of "Coronation Street"—are among the admissions every week. We have retained our preliminary notes from one day last year because they are typical of the folk seeking asylum every day. We ourselves saw all these new admissions in one morning and see similar folk many mornings in the year.

1. Mrs. A., 36, European nationality, married to a senior business executive, three young children and an au pair girl, also runs her own business, good holidays abroad (she looked very suntanned for mid-winter), some contact with the local church, very dependent on her mother.

2. Mr. B., 19, student, attempted suicide, says he gets on all right with parents and brother, keeps up with studies satisfactorily, regular girl friend, nice-looking lad. Why did he attempt suicide? "I couldn't stand the loneliness of life any longer."

3. Mr. C., 35, West Indian, three years in Britain, labourer, no family or friends here, cannot hold down jobs for more than two to three weeks, calls himself a wanderer, says we have no idea of the hell it is to be black in Britain.

4. Miss D., 19, student, only child, criminally assaulted at 10, parents cultured, educated, sent her to fee-paying schools, they won't accept that she cannot make the grade and cannot keep up with other students, frightened of everyone, strong church background.

5. Mrs. E., 24, two young children, husband attacks her and hits her regularly, in front of children, says she is mental, gets on well with rest of family, difficult to cope with babies' washing, yesterday husband punched her in the face for not having lunch ready and she went for him with a knife. . . .

6. Mr. F., 24, parents had just brought him in, very agitated, shaking violently all over, stood in a crouch position and said he could not move: "it" has got him. . . .

These are folk all under 40; all but one was discharged within a month, with every possibility that they will not need re-admission. The chances of recovery, especially among younger people, are very good. Some folk are just old and lonely and often there is a shortage of beds because the local authorities (and Ministry of Health) are using mental hospitals as geriatric hospitals as well.

A recent survey shows that very nearly one in three patients attending family doctors did so predominantly for psychiatric reasons. There can be no doubt that greater emphasis should be placed on the teaching of psychiatry to medical and theological students, specially in the opportunities for relieving anxiety in people. We said deliberately that many folk are "victims"—victims of unhappy childhood, of H.P., of loneliness, of divorced parents, of colour, of war, of success, of vice. We find that very few of the circumstances seem to be the patient's own fault or responsibility. Those who are not victims of divorce, status, colour, loneliness or vice have more to be thankful for than we shall ever realise. Yesterday morning a woman patient broke down during Holy Communion and cried for the entire service. She was shrieking, "*It's a year ago today that my daughter was murdered*".

The "top problem" in mental illness is perhaps the community. Many mental patients have no near relatives and no visitors, and folk are not prepared to commit themselves to after-care visiting and help. Thus many "out-patients" relapse, returning to the loneliness and anxieties of a life which may have partly caused the illness in the first place. There are several wards in our hospital, each with 30–35 patients, where the patients hardly ever get a single visitor. No one cares. We ourselves have often tracked down families living within a mile of the hospital and begged them to visit a patient they have not visited for months or years—*their own parent or child*. Or again, we have to bury patients : *rarely is there even one mourner*.

People who have been mentally ill do not get enough of the support they need once they have been discharged from hospital. There is not nearly enough help and guidance for friends and relatives looking after them. Considering that one family in five throughout Britain has one member suffering from a serious mental disorder which means hospital treatment, this is a sad deficiency. The social stigma of having been in a place of rest and refuge—an asylum—is dying slowly and the general public, relatives and even health workers are still, in some cases, ignorant and afraid of mental illness. Particularly is this apparent when the patient comes home.

Life can be very cruel to men and women trying to resume their place in the community. This is often the biggest worry among in-patients and it sometimes is a terrifying experience after the shelter and calm of hospital routine ; even the noise of life outside is an ordeal. A great deal is done at the hospital end to help with rehabilitation : patients go home for the day and then for weekends before discharge, and some go out to a normal job and return each night and all those discharged receive regular supervision as out-patients. Twenty-five years ago patients with serious mental illness had only a two in five chance of ever leaving hospital, but now four out of five of them spend most of their time at home, often at work, though requiring periods of readmission from time to time. The need for asylums will never disappear, but the chances of recovery are now so good that the Ministry of Health dares to hope for a 50 per cent reduction in mental hospital beds over the next 10 years. But rehabilitation is not easy. Last Saturday a young staff nurse, a keen Christian, went back to duty after treatment with us. Her first job was to report to matron after two months' sick leave. Matron said in a biting voice "We all know where you've been. It's time you did some work after all this holidaying". As she walked down the corridor the staff nurse had her first encounter with another nurse—"So they've let you out" was all the nurse said as they passed. It was enough. *The staff nurse was back as a mental patient by lunch-time.*

A note of caution must be sounded here. We still know very little about mental disorders. We ourselves are frequently confronted by "ordinary" normal folks in our mental hospital and they baffle us. We listen and probe and try to find out what brings them inside, and even after staff consultation, we are often none the wiser, though few of us are ready to admit this. Psychiatry in 1966 is still a new field of enquiry and study, and we are frequently baffled by people. Pressure of time is another factor in psychiatric treatment. There are so many who need help and counselling and even if the number of beds required may decrease, the number of out-patient sessions is rising rapidly. How many of us realise that in actual practice *full* psychoanalysis demands not less than three to five interviews a week for anything from two to four years?

Why pray when we can worry? Today there are, for example, many more people worrying themselves to distraction about the possibility of suffering from syphilis or tuberculosis or cancer than there are patients whose mental life is impaired by the physical effect of these conditions upon the cells of their brains. Illness and dis-ease of all kinds are undeniably important in the production of suffering, anxiety and unhappiness. In general terms it is not so much the particular nature of the stress, whether it be external disaster or internal damage or disease, which is of supreme importance, but rather how a person faced by this stress feels about it himself. Ultimately mental illness is an extremely personal form of suffering.

No survey of mental health, however brief, would be complete without reference to parents and parenthood. Every approach to the preventative aspect of mental illness tends logically and inevitably to focus attention upon the health and happiness of children. The patterns of behaviour acquired by adults are laid down in childhood and our whole personality and constitution are an intimate blend of hereditary factors and the effects upon us of our environment from the very earliest years of life. There can be no substitute for a happy home—as we tell all godparents and parents at baptisms. We listen to patient after patient with a deep compassion for the child whom we have never known, but who is now before us, physically grown but emotionally starved or stunted, outwardly mature but inwardly anxious, tense, unhappy and a prey to that insecurity which is the enemy of calm and contentment. This is especially true of "war babies" who have now grown into young men and women of 19 to 25. They seem to have a higher rate of sex problems and are more emotionally vulnerable than other generations. The trouble has sprung from fathers being away at the battle front, mothers having to bring up children under "hardship" conditions, evacuation, and a higher proportion of babies than usual being unwanted.

In a mental hospital we see something of the "new morality" at first hand. We doubt whether men and women flout convention as easily as is generally supposed. Everyone without exception has a conscience and a capacity to feel guilty. We tell our Church youngsters that anyone who thinks that adultery, fornication, venereal disease, illegitimate children, sexual free-for-all can be happily indulged and shrugged off without consequence, ought to have a spell in a mental hospital or teenagers' "worry clinic". The "victims" would soon convince them of the consequences. Some of the folk we ourselves have counselled range from teenage mothers shot through with guilt complexes to older men and women who committed sexual irregularities *20 or 30 years ago* and still have them on their conscience.

Of course not everyone who commits fornication or contacts V.D. will end up in an asylum, but some do: and even those who are more fortunate find that they do not dismiss the mental consequences as easily as they imagine. We leave mental health by posing a true situation, which perhaps exists many times over, with the invitation to consider the implications of the situation in terms both of mental health and of parenthood, past and future. The girl in question could easily live in our town, our street, next door or in our own homes. This is her problem:

"My boy friend and I are very much in love but my attractive girl friend is making me miserable. She is experienced with boys and has told me she would like to go to bed with my boy friend.

He has also admitted he feels an overwhelming desire for her, but he doesn't want to hurt me. We can't avoid her, so what can I do? I must add that my boy and I have sexual inter- course regularly, which makes his desire for her all the more puzzling."

From fornication and all other deadly sin; and from all deceits of the world, the flesh and the devil, Good Lord, deliver us.

SUICIDE

No one can give a straightforward and general answer to the question "What makes a man or woman take his or her own life?". Reasons for suicide vary so much from person to person (and how can we be sure?). In the United Kingdom an average of 7000 people commit suicide each year and in the U.S. the figure is 18,000. If we were to include the number of suicides from countries overseas, the final figure would be staggering. The rate for Austria is 24.9 per hundred thousand of population, for Denmark 23.5, for Finland 22.9, for Switzerland 22.6 and for Sweden 21.1. It is perhaps an encouraging reflection on the Welfare State and on "the Dynamic Society" that our own rates in 1965 were 12.3 and 11.4 per hundred thousand.

But this is not all. It has been reliably ascertained that the number of unsuccessful suicide attempts of varying degree of determination is probably 10 times as great as the number of "successful" suicides. Five million people living in the United States today have at some time attempted to kill themselves. Most attempts fail but one in five eventually succeeds. A woman of 35, beset by domestic troubles in the middle of the week, is the person most likely to commit suicide. Suicidal depression seems to be most intense on Wednesday nights, with domestic trouble as the main cause. Women suicides outnumber men and the average age is 35. This was stated in a report to the American Psychiatric Association. And in Britain there are some 500,000 people who have attempted suicide. These figures represent an appalling sum of woe, desperation and loneliness in the midst of Western prosperity. Social factors are the main cause in 39 per cent of suicide attempts, followed by physical illness in 18 per cent. Of those who succeed it is maintained that 45 per cent have psychiatric problems, but what is more disturbing is that 55 per cent would probably not have taken their lives had they received non-medical counselling or the support of loving friends and relations, or both. Meanwhile doctors and others may ponder the fact that taking an overdose of tablets is now the most popular method.

More American teenagers are committing suicide. Often they may be driven to suicide by something as apparently trivial as a telling off by a teacher. Ten years ago suicide was the fifth most common cause of death in the 15 to 19 age group: now it is in third place. Another puzzling phenomenon is the recent increase in the number of suicides among Negroes. Since 1946 the suicide rate of Negro men has doubled. It is even more significant that of the thousand Negro suicides each year, two-thirds take place in the financially secure, even wealthy, group. For as the Negro wins his way into the material plenty of American middle- and upper-class life, he inherits economic, social and psychological tensions possessed by his white counterparts.

The number of drug suicides in Britain went up from 787 to 1083 last year. This is very worrying because it is probable that more and more people are becoming emotionally and physically dependent on barbiturate drugs. The suicide rate from taking barbiturates has increased *ten-fold* in the last 15 years. Despite constant warnings in the medical press of the dangers of addiction, the consumption of drugs and with it the increasing number of suicides both actual and attempted and of fatal accidents continues to rise alarmingly. Figures show that the quantity of barbiturate drugs prescribed by general practitioners under the National Health Service has trebled in the past 10 years. It is difficult to arrive at a firm figure for attempted drug suicides; but if the normal rates in estimates is adhered to it means that attempted suicides by barbiturates is now about 8000–10,000 each year. These drugs and tablets can be "killers" and one of the worries of those concerned with care of the mentally ill is that those who keep "attempting" suicide will one day try once too often and succeed by *accident*.

The high suicide rate among undergraduates is very per-plexing. University days are intended to be happy and exciting and creative. Oxford and Cambridge have a suicide rate of five times the national average for the 20–24 age group. There is a tendency to blame university staff for not finding out whether undergraduates have personal problems; however it would seem reasonable to expect students of that age to be capable of seeking help and advice when they need it. Perhaps the abolition of military service is depriving undergraduates of the benefit of wider experience, stability and responsibility. In "our day" we were commissioned at 18 and commanding troops, and went up as fresh*men* alongside others who were Korea veterans or who had been in action in South East Asia. Perhaps our problem was not that we would have wished college staff to come enquir-ing into our emotional stability, but that after military respon-sibility it was tempting to resent such college discipline and supervision as was necessarily imposed by staff who knew little of life beyond university confines. Nevertheless last year the *New Cambridge* magazine carried out large-scale student surveys which discovered that 46 per cent of undergraduates worried about sex, 42 per cent about work, 36 per cent about their future and 19 per cent about their family. Practically all students had fits of deep depression. These surveys also indicated that the types most likely to develop suicidal tendencies were the gram-mar school boy from a working-class background and the public school boy—which covers the majority of students at British universities. It seems necessary to follow the wise example of American institutions and provide adequate psychologists for the mental care of students. Perhaps we now need "worry clinics" at Oxford and Cambridge.

DRINK

The drink menace is another world-wide problem . . . but it casts its darkest shadows in the West. Convictions for drunken-ness have increased by 60 per cent in the past decade, and each adult in this country now consumes on average four bottles of spirits a year; this is the highest consumption rate for 40 years. There are an estimated 400,000 alcoholics in Britain today, of whom one in five is a woman. And alcoholism is costing industry £30–£40 million every year. But the problem is not at all simple. It is not by any means easy to define alcoholism. Some people can drink vastly more than others without disrupting their working or family life. Even if the alcoholic can be defined as one so addicted to alcohol that he cannot do without it, it is impossible to suggest any social legislation which will secure him against temptation without serious invasion of the rights of moderate drinkers.

In the United States there are about 2 million alcoholics on the payrolls of business and industry, and they cost their managements more than 1 billion dollars annually through absenteeism. American spending on alcoholic beverages is rising at the annual rate of £185 million. In 1965 Americans spent over £50,000 million on alcoholic beverages of all types—more than they spent on petrol and oil for their cars. It has been observed that countries confronted with almost any other problem of this magnitude would have long since declared themselves to be in the throes of a crisis of epidemic proportions.

An alcoholic is ill, very ill, and in need of treatment. He *cannot* "snap out of it" without help, and anyone of any age or background is liable to become a victim of chronic alcoholism. Fortunately it is now regarded as a treatable disease—with a possible 70 per cent success rate—and a world-wide health problem. It is one of the most serious health and social problems confronting any industrial country and certainly one of the most expensive. We know that it is a killer on the roads, taking toll of thousands of lives. How many of the *57,500 killed last year* in America and Britain would be alive today had it not been for drunken drivers? We have to be eternally vigilant. At the beginning of Christmas Week 1964 in the midst of the Government's £479,000 "Don't Drink and Drive Campaign" we had a new by-pass opened on the outskirts of this town. It was opened by the Joint Parliamentary Secretary to the Ministry of Transport and in his speech he said "don't drink and drive". The press photograph of the ceremony showed him *drinking*.

Alcoholism is a common cause of "impaired" and drunken driving; over 50 per cent of alcoholic car drivers have admitted court appearances for drunken driving. It has been found that with those who admitted habitual driving in an impaired condition, this had occurred quite early in their drinking "career", on the average with men in the late 20s or early 30s.

In the U.S. one out of every 13 drinkers eventually became an alcoholic. A comprehensive American study published by Rutgers University at the end of 1964 dashes for ever the theory that drinking is the curse of the working-class. It is well known that Americans (and Britons) as a nation drink too much, but this latest survey reveals the remarkable fact that the highest drinking rate (87 per cent) is among those earning £3500 or more. In contrast, only 54 per cent of those earning the lowest wages of less than £1000 a year drink. So much for the old story of the workman squandering his meagre pay in the corner pub. The social investigators point out moreover that 89 per cent of the population with college degrees drink, compared with only 46 per cent of those whose education stopped at elementary school level. Heaviest drinkers, they say, are lawyers, judges, doctors, dentists and college presidents.

It is probably true to say that something under 5 per cent of major mental disorder is directly and solely due to alcohol, but it is equally likely that alcoholism is one of the most potent single causes of unhappiness among families, of broken homes, of minor and major crime, and particularly of violence and homicidal attacks, and that not a few of the behaviour disturbances seen in children and the character disorders which may cripple the lives of adults owe a great deal to alcoholic addiction, not primarily on the part of the patient but on the part of one or both of the parents. Teenage drunkenness is rising rapidly.

Alcoholism is considered to be the fourth greatest public health problem, ranking with cancer, heart disease and mental illness. Certainly it is a major Transatlantic problem. And the amount of manhours lost in both countries, attributable to alcohol, makes a staggering total.

CRIME

What puzzles and dismays so many about crime today is that its rate steadily advances as living standards rise. Why is this happening? With the highest standard of living in our history there were committed in 1965 well over a million indictable offences known to the police. Crime in America's suburbs rose by 20 per cent last year compared with 1964; the biggest element in the suburban crime increase was a 33 per cent rise in the number of rapes. The overall increase in crime in the U.S. in 1965 was 13 per cent. These figures are from a report from the Director of the Federal Bureau of Investigation.

Every hour of the day 300 serious crimes are committed in America. Of those solved, 37 per cent involved boys under 18. Since 1958 crime has been rising six times as fast as the population. The crime breakdown is: a murder every hour, a rape every 26 minutes, assault every three minutes, robbery every five minutes, burglary every 28 seconds, grand larceny every 45 seconds and a car theft a minute. So serious is the crime rate that President Johnson set up a national crime commission in 1965, which is spending eighteen months investigating the causes of crime, ways of improving police standards and fresh ideas on rehabilitating juvenile and adult offenders.

These international figures are more than a paradox, they are appalling. They bear not on our productivity, our balance of trade, our capacity to defend ourselves, all of which we worry about a good deal, but on the sort of people we are becoming. It is small comfort to know that other prosperous industrial societies are steadily growing more dishonest. Worse, there is some evidence that the million-plus offences of 1965 do not fully account for our dishonesty. Lots of property offences were not reported at all. A survey suggests that employers increasingly condone theft—though they may distinguish between stealing money (bad) and pilfering (not so bad)—to avoid unpleasantness, adverse publicity and, in full employment, the difficulty of filling vacancies. In the years immediately before the war Britain could expect 3000 cases of personal violence a year—the figure is now over 20,000. Even the comparatively short period between 1960 and 1964 saw a rise in the number of breaking and entering cases from 151,000 to 229,000. Today British women and girls run a one in 2000 risk each year of being indecently assaulted. Many New York women carry tear-gas protection, and Governor

Rockefeller signed a Bill requiring every flat in New York City to have a peephole in the front door to enable a tenant to identify callers. This law is a step towards reducing criminal assaults on New Yorkers in their homes.

Crime costs Britain at least £225 million each year. The value of stolen property last year was put at £30 million; pilfering in industry and commerce was estimated to account for £70 million and £125 million covered police costs in tracking criminals and the bills for the prison service. We have 29,000 prisoners—the first decrease since 1956—costing £11 16s. 4d. a week in 1965. There were 477 escapes from gaol last year and 900 boys absconded from borstal institutions. The treatment of a persistent delinquent from the age of 10 to 24 costs the community about £8000. A typical modern rake's progress begins with two periods of probation before going on to an approved school, borstal and finally prison. His place in a remand home costs £24 a week, approved school £18 a week, borstal £14 a week and prison almost £12. Other problems might be his illegitimate child, National Assistance for his wife and children, and accommodation for the family following eviction. The falling success rate of remedial institutions is a perplexing problem.

It is no longer true to say that crime does not pay—at least in material terms. Take something from a parked car in London and the chances of being caught are less than one in 10. The risk is greater with shops or warehouses but only a fifth of such cases are "cleared up". London policemen track down only a third of the burglars, a tenth of the pedal-cycle stealers and a fifth of the car-takers. The equivalent of one week's car production is stolen in London each year; 85 per cent are recovered but most of these are damaged. In West Germany legislation compels manufacturers to fit mechanical anti-theft locks on all vehicles, and in Scandinavia insurance companies refuse to insure vehicles not fitted with an approved safety device.

Criminals with a more brutal turn of mind have much less chance. Over three-quarters of the nation's rapists are caught and the success rate against murderers is very much higher. In Washington, D.C. 139 of last year's record 140 murders were solved. Looking at Britain as a whole the criminal fares better

H

if he works in London, for the metropolis clears up only a fifth of its crimes each year. In the provinces the police success is somewhat higher and the national average is 39 per cent. Crime in this town during 1965 soared to a record-breaking figure—crimes averaged more than 12 a day—and was almost double the 1960 figure; but 56 per cent of last year's crime was detected. Although these figures would seem to indicate a pretty bright future for crime and a fairly bleak one for us victims, it is perhaps some comfort to know that as crime gets more serious so the chance of getting away becomes more limited.

One of the difficulties holding up the police in their efforts is the fact that no one seems to know why people become criminals. The popular theory that the rate of crime is in direct proportion to the numbers of unemployed has been destroyed utterly. But there can be little doubt about what age they do it. In Britain three youths in every hundred between the ages of 14 and 17 are found guilty of indictable offences each year. An interesting experiment in the punishment and cure of juvenile delinquency is being conducted in a Chicago suburb. There the job of sentencing young people found guilty by a magistrate of such offences as shop-lifting, vandalism and traffic violations has been entrusted to a Youth Jury. This consists of six high school pupils drawn from a panel of 45. Punishments are designed to fit the crime. Thus offenders may be ordered to mow lawns, sweep the streets, work as an orderly in a hospital or clean up public buildings. If they have been found guilty of theft they are sentenced to earn enough money to make restitution. They cannot get it from their parents. A youth officer on the local police force decides which cases should go before the Youth Jury after studying the record of the offender and interviewing the parents. Offenders then have the choice of being sentenced by the magistrate or submitting themselves to the Youth Jury. If they opt for the second alternative, they avoid getting a police record and so far all offenders have submitted to the Youth Jury. So far 80 cases have been handled in this manner and none of the young people involved has been in trouble a second time. Acts of teenage vandalism are decreasing. The key to the success of the system is the fact that judgment is passed by members of the younger generation.

A recently-retired High Court Judge said last week, "I would say without hesitation that incomparably the greatest cause of serious crime in this country is excessive drinking". However, the more we reflect the more we hesitate and sense that there are many other causes and that prosperity may be one of them. Our society sets great store by economic affluence and social ascent. This is true both sides of the Atlantic. Yet our communities contain many who cannot attain those ends by legitimate means. The solution is "innovation" and where material wealth is involved that means fraud, embezzlement, vice, theft and blackmail.

There seems to be no limit to criminal ingenuity. We mused on this during our "prosperity spot" this week when the car was being washed at a car-wash firm (perhaps the only time we sit in affluence watching others work!). Another local car-wash firm has introduced a new type of ticket this week—they were losing over £1000 weekly through forged tickets at their branches! Thus it seems that a "successful" society will generate the strains that lead to crime among the weakest. *The faster the "rat race" the more tempting it becomes for little rats to cut the corners.*

This is a melancholy prospect for societies dedicated to growth, expansion and yet higher standards of living. Must we accept that prosperity inevitably cultivates dishonesty?

HOLIDAY FROM SEX?

Obsession with sex is likely to strike future historians as one of the outstanding characteristics of contemporary society. In its cruder manifestations it shows itself in the practice and encouragement of promiscuity, uninhibited and shameless. This open encouragement is without parallel since the late and degenerate period of the old pagan civilisation which Christianity fought to overcome. More subtly, the same obsession is to be seen in the great range of commercial advertising and in much of modern literature and dramatic art.

Man must have something or somebody to worship. In the vacuum left for millions by the rebellion against the worship of God, the most natural thing in the world is for his rightful place to be taken by the powers and pleasures connected with sex. These formed the staple of the ancient pagan religions. Once the Christian guard is lowered, the way is wide open to the return of the old dark divinities. The modern devotees of sexual indulgence do not think of themselves as religious at all; they pride themselves on having put aside all such childish things. Yet they look for some source of satisfaction which will lift them above themselves, some power to which they can accord priority in their lives. And they find it in the deepest of human emotional experiences. To all intents and purposes they worship sex.

Thank God that for millions and millions, indeed for the majority, sex is good and pure and confined within the marriage bond. Happy homes and families do not hit the headlines; yet they make good news, namely, that marriage and sex and family life are gifts from God which He intends us to use and enjoy. And it needs stressing again and again that most married couples find that sex is the wonderful gift that God intended it to be. Most teenagers grow up without catching venereal disease or begetting illegitimate offspring. Certainly sexual perversion and promiscuity are increasing; nevertheless these vices still apply to the minority of the population.

At the same time there is no cause for optimism. Sex is an obsession. Modern Christians cannot ignore this situation. We have to react to it one way or another. Some Christians favour a withdrawal of the Church from a world largely given over to vice and perversion, so that we can be free to concentrate on our own spiritual duties and our own distinctive way of life. But this cannot be the way of those who believe in the Incarnation and are called to be servants of the saving Cross. God so loves *this* world. Some now leap to the other extreme and advocate so thorough an involvement with the world that they seem eager to abandon all Christian standards. The Swedish Lutheran Church is to set up a special commission to reconsider a pronouncement made in 1959 which branded pre-marital sexual relationships as a sin. A spokesman said that the commission would study whether this pronouncement should be modified in view of a widely-discussed demand that the Church align itself more closely to "reality". This world will never be won over by people of God who are simply willing to go the way of the world, in the anxiety to avoid giving offence. It is surely of the utmost importance for the very survival of the Christian witness and way of life that Church members acquaint themselves with trends in sex behaviour and acquire some sense of where the responsibilities lie. Sex today is causing suffering, personal anxiety, distress and even tragedy in countless homes. Christians cannot contract out. There *may* be some of today's fornicators and adulterers who will go into the kingdom of Heaven before us. To scold or to blame is valueless, but how can we pass by on the other side when sex is all round us? Is it without significance that Jesus was betrayed with a kiss?

Consider these facts:

1. *Last year 150,000 new patients attended V.D. clinics in Britain. In America 1500 boys and girls catch V.D. every day, the Surgeon-General reported. These venereal- and sexually-transmitted diseases, in retreat in the 1950s after the introduction of penicillin, are again a major health problem on a world scale, especially among young people. Immigrants account for 53%.*

2. *Divorce proceedings rose to over 40,000 last year: it is impossible to calculate the total number of people caught up in divorce —parents, teenagers, young children, relatives and friends. Both Britain and America now have Divorcees Anonymous and the U.S. has one divorce for every four marriages p.a.*

3. *In a survey carried out among 7000 of Britain's 23,000 family doctors 38 per cent approved of instruction in contraception techniques for teenagers.*

4. *There are now two London birth control clinics for young unmarried people. The staff are working overtime and the waiting list for selected applicants is two months.*

5. *More than 2 million American girls between 13–17 are married every year. Teenage marriage is a major social problem with millions plunging in without thought for their financial and emotional future. American fashion catalogues list maternity dresses in sizes for "misses" and "juniors".*

6. *Last year there were 37 cases of V.D. in children of 14, 235 among 15-year-olds, and 1357 among 16-year-olds. Almost all these cases were grammar school children.*

7. *Two out of three babies born to girls under 20 are conceived out of wedlock: every thirteenth baby is a bastard. It is now estimated that two out of every three single girls reaching the age of 25 are no longer virgins.*

8. *Medical specialists estimate that 4–6 per cent of all men are practising homosexuals and a similar proportion of women are lesbian: one in 20 of everyone we know.*

9. *Every day there are about 300 illegal abortions. This adds up to at least 100,000 every year. About 150 are performed annually under the National Health Service, and this might be more if women knew their rights in this matter. In an illegal back-street abortion the dangers of infection, permanent injury, mental stress and death are very considerable. At least one woman dies like this every week. A recent T.V. programme interviewed teenage students who had three abortions.*

10. *The 1965 Report of the Central Council for Health Education says two-thirds of boys and three-quarters of girls know at the age of 13 or think they know the facts of life. At 14 years of age, one boy in 50 and less than one girl in 200 are sexually experienced. It is not until the age of 17 that one boy in four and one girl in eight, and by 19 that one boy in three and one girl in four have had sexual experience. Intercourse usually takes place at home.*

11. *In court last month the magistrates were told that a man who advertised obscene photographs for sale received £11,000 in two days from men aged 22 to 76, sending from £2 to £60. Amongst the obscene literature seized by the police last year were 579,000 pin-up magazines, 401,000 paperbacks and 85,000 photographs and negatives.*

12. *The president of the Students' Union at one of our "modern" universities announced that there was no reason why contraceptives should not be sold in the Union Shop. The Vice-*

Chancellor intervened. Later the president—a 20-year-old student—stated his intervention was wholly unreasonable and unacceptable.

13. *Dr. Leslie Weatherhead has recently reported of 18 girls going up to university a year ago. Within three months 13 had lost their virginity. One university girl had told him, "You are asked to come to a cocktail party, but you know that means 'sleep me with afterwards'. Men use us as they use the lavatory".*

14. *Dr. Weatherhead also spoke of a class of 14-year-olds, of which 25 per cent of the girls admitted sexual intercourse with more than one person. "We are", he said, with regard to sexual intercourse, "verging on a national disaster".*

15. *Sexual promiscuity among young people is now so commonplace says a chief constable's annual report, that if every case of unlawful sexual intercourse with girls under 16 was brought to trial the courts would be overloaded.*

16. *"Sex at School" was featured in a recent issue of the Family Planning journal and a 17-year-old girl claimed that about a third of the sixth-form girls at her school were no longer virgins and that many boys regarded use of contraceptives as "chicken".*

Is there more promiscuity among young people today than there was 50 or 100 years ago? There is no way of finding a certain answer to this question. But the statistics that are available for the rapid increase in the treatment of venereal disease and the greater number of illegitimate babies and pre-marital conception strongly suggests that during the fifties and sixties young people have become more promiscuous. Evidence from young people themselves, from social workers, clergy, police and probation officers and others closely connected with the young make it clear that pre-marital and extra-marital intercourse is now common. Presumably some of these people attend church regularly.

But what has prosperity to do with promiscuity? Can we be sure that there is any definite connection? Let us look more closely at some of the apparent causes of our obsession with sex.

Group behaviour is a cause, and the pressure to conform is extremely strong in an affluent society. A young and inexperienced girl or boy may consent to intercourse because they do not want to be different from their friends. All-night parties are a sex-trap for many innocent young people and they can end up in a V.D. clinic. Group behaviour does not grip only the young and innocent. There is the same problem at universities and colleges on both sides of the Atlantic. It is being said that an increasing number of students regard sexual relations as essential to their education. "Everything but—" seems the common practice: this is not chastity or virginity in the Christian sense.

Family life is a cause. The breakdown of the family as a unit frequently strains communication between one generation and another. In a time of such prosperity family life and loyalties are subjected to considerable economic and social pressures, and this can lead to friction between parents and children. Today there is a growing tendency for a household to go their own way and live in corporate isolation from each other. Many parents are shirking their responsibilities. Young girls do become pregnant or contract venereal disease because of their parents who fail to supervise their activities adequately or who are unwilling to make the sacrifices which such chaperonage involves.

Yes, parents can be a cause—by their own example and lack of supervision. We know parents who go away for the weekend when their children have parties. Parents who go out and leave young people alone to have parties are exposing them to great temptation because they do drink and can become irresponsible. It seems quite the usual thing in certain societies to have sexual intercourse somewhere about the house. Wise are the parents of teenagers who go out to the cinema but return at the reasonable hour of 10.30 to 11 p.m. thus combining independence with supervision when it begins to get late or tempting. At our sixth-form or prefects' social activities the head always asked "What time do you want me to come back?"

What about a youth curfew? With teenagers committing a major share of American crimes, the Gallup Poll has conducted a survey on ways and means of combating this problem. Of those questioned, 77 per cent believe it would be a good idea to impose a teenage curfew. Many communities already have such a law. In Philadelphia, for example, youths under 17 must be in their homes by 10.30 p.m. on week-nights and Sundays, and by midnight of Fridays and Saturdays.

It is good to know that many teachers and parents, indeed the vast majority, are encouraging strict moral standards. A group of Oxford parents is concerned at the number of mental break-downs and the incidence of promiscuity, abortion and drug-taking at Oxford University, all of which are increasing, they say in written evidence to the Franks Commission. Nevertheless it may be equally true that parents and grown-ups go too far these days. A National paper described a typical 1966 party given by respectable, middle-class people in an affluent suburb— "There was a 'have you heard this one' group. Everyone, men and women, roared hugely at a joke involving the liberal use of a four-letter word. A man put his arm round the waist of some-body else's pretty wife, kissed her on the mouth and told her she was a sexy thing. Then he also told her in the clearest possible terms why he had to go out of the room for a short while."

A few years ago such behaviour would have been breaking all the rules in the party book. One New York hotel manager says that he does not care if an unmarried couple sign the register as man and wife. What does anger him is that a man takes a room as a single occupant and then brings a woman in —thus cheating the hotel of its revenue. We have just had a case in the assizes here of nine men accused of offences against a girl. The men's ages ranged from 19 to 70, four were over 50, and three had children of their own. The offences had been going on regularly for over 18 months and the judge described the girl as "a pretty skilful temptress of the most horrible type and nothing short of a little prostitute". At the time the offences started *she was just 13*. Yes, grown-ups are as responsible as teenagers for our present moral standards.

Advertising is a cause. And this includes television. There is too much sex and violence on T.V., though we doubt whether this is as widespread as some critics and Church groups main-tain. Perhaps the Clean Up T.V. Movement founded in Feb-ruary, 1964, is making itself felt; it now claims 300,000 members. The following chart shows in percentages how 15,000 viewers voted on the T.V. issues:

	Not true	Very true	Partly true
Too much sex	38	41	21
Too much violence	44	34	22
Too much seamy side	45	31	24
Too much bad language	53	27	20

General advertising is colossal: in 1965 we are spending almost £600 million—45 per cent on press advertising, 18 per cent on T.V., 8 per cent on catalogues, leaflets, and the remainder on window displays, samples and gift schemes. Advertising is £4800 million annual business in the United States, bigger than steel (£3700 million). Even in the U.K. the advertising business was a bigger business than computers (£42.6 million), shipbuilding (£105.7 million), machine tools (£121 million) and aircraft (£110 million) put together. Most of this advertising does not attempt to convince us rationally. It appeals instead to certain deep level emotions. Take any group of advertisements and see how many of them try to "get" us in one of these ways: snob appeal, exploitation, money for nothing, sex and fear. Sex and fear are sure winners in advertising. Much of this advertising is directed towards teenagers. Last year almost £30 million was spent on drink advertising, mainly directed towards young people. In one survey of 2600 V.D. patients, alcohol had been taken by 77 per cent of the males and 25 per cent of the females before having intercourse which led to infection. In Denmark the state T.V. to schools now tells children where and how contraceptives can be bought and used. In Britain nearly £2 million is spent on advertising *every day*. Depth psychology in many forms of advertising persuades us that social success is measured in terms of sexual success. Commercial exploitation of sex drives—not the call-girls—is our most serious form of prostitution today. A schoolgirl said "Your parents tell you not to, but the films, magazines, advertising posters and records all present such a glamorous and attractive picture of sex that you want to know what it is all about, and of course, it is the first step that counts".

Affluence is a cause. Plenty of money, cars, time, independence and opportunities, and teenagers are sorely tempted to find sin fun. A recent British Medical Association report took up and questioned the idea that "the ease with which it is possible to buy contraceptives makes it easier for young people to have sexual intercourse". Yet a study of 160 young people with V.D. indicated that only one in six took precautions. Ten of the boys had had intercourse with too many girls to count and never used contraceptives. Think of the probable tragedies in countless homes and families. Teenage girls who have had *three* abortions say that it is because boys refuse to use contraceptives. The oral contraceptive is gaining ground fast. Users have risen to about 600,000, an increase of 350 per cent in two and a half years. The pills cost about 10s. for a month's supply at normal retail prices. One expert in venereal diseases has predicted a Black Market in these pills in 1966–67 in girls' grammar schools. If more liberal use of the birth control pill leads to increased promiscuity there will almost certainly be a great upsurge in venereal disease, against which the pill provides no protection.

If we think that the subject of contraceptives and young people is not vexing all sections of the community, we deceive ourselves and the truth is not in us. Next week we have to "pontificate" at a Deanery Federation brains trust of the Church of England Men's Society; we have been warned that one question will be: "Should fathers give instructions to their sons on the use of contraceptives (as protection against V.D. and illegitimate children)?". Let us make no mistake: *Christian* people are being confronted by these situations in their own homes and ordinary circumstances. We cannot leave this distressing subject without noting that even if a contraceptive is invented which is entirely effective and even if venereal diseases can be eliminated by medical means, then a serious spiritual and moral problem will still exist.

Sex is the key to colour tension in America. How many would accept this? This is the conclusion of a penetrating and extensive programme of research by sociologists to get to the root cause of colour tension in the United States. This report *Sex and Racism in America*, published in 1965, lays the blame for race hatred on the sexual tensions created artificially in the Deep South. The Southern white man, it states, is obsessed by the idea of the Negro desiring sexual relations with white women. In his turn the Negro is secretly tormented every second of his waking life by the presence of white women in his midst whom he must not touch. "On the other hand the white man cannot adhere to his own laws prohibiting inter-racial intercourse. He insults, seduces and rapes black women as if this is what they exist for . . ." And many Southern women seem to have an almost obsessive preoccupation with rape—although statistics prove that she is more likely to be struck by lightning than assaulted by a Negro. Cases are cited to show that Southern white women are not only sexually attracted to the barred Negroes but are actually the aggressors where sexual relationships are concerned. Many of these tensions have their roots back in the guilt and fear born in the days of slavery on the Southern plantations. Perhaps the saddest thing revealed by this investigation is that there seems to be no solution in sight. "From all indications our sons and daughters, and their sons and daughters in turn, will be victimised by the American sexual nightmare."

Of course our concern can go to the extreme and become an obsession. When Christians do this, they fashion sex into something quite the reverse of what God intends it to be. For example, in one European country there is considerable national controversy as to whether "eye-catching legs cost manhours". Some industrialists are concerned that shorter skirts are costing the nation a large sum in gazing time. To combat the risk of consequent money lost some banks have imposed stiff regulations on what employees must wear, including a "suitable length skirt". On the other hand some companies believe women's natural beauty to be an asset likely to attract clients. One of the nation's major airlines, for instance, recently ordered skirts to be shortened for air hostesses. We should feel that national controversy about attractive legs is a typical obsession which Christians, at least, could do well to avoid.

Yet there must be Christian compassion, concern and enquiry.

How often do we pray individually or collectively for those who are divorced, illegitimate, prostitutes, childless, adulterers, promiscuous teenagers? An honest Christian will admit that he rarely, if ever, lifts up society in this way to the Father's care and with the prayer, "There but for the grace of God go I".

We often speak as though adultery, venereal disease and promiscuity were the only problems in sex. This is not so. We have already mentioned mental disturbance as one major factor in the loosening of moral standards. There are other problems, not connected with moral behaviour. Many a psychiatrist, parish priest and marriage guidance counsellor will know from experience the heartbreak of childlessness and the sterility of one partner. There are also the special problems of the single person, unmarried perhaps because no one has asked him or her. There are the problems of adoption. Most of these spheres of concern are apparently beneath the surface, but only just. Think about the 70,000 children in the care of local authorities, growing up without the love of parents and the security of their own homes. Leave aside the fact that this costs ratepayers £27 million in 1965. We do not know what proportion of these children were orphans, but it is probably not high. We have worked in a large children's home : at no time did the proportion of orphans (both parents dead) rise to 5 per cent, and more than 80 per cent had both parents alive—but separated or divorced. We know something too about the tensions of adoption. We know one couple, happily married, who would dearly love children of their own, who finally adopted a little son. After several weeks of the "trial" period had elapsed, the real mother changed her mind and wanted the child back. The journey itself was 300 miles each way. Two days later the mother said she did not want the child. Back the couple went. The present position is that they are still "on trial" and will have to go to court to get a legal order and the real mother has again indicated that she is not prepared to sign the child off her hands. It is beyond us to describe the tension and tragedy of this situation. Do we love him as our own or will he be taken from us? What effect will this have on his personality and mental stability?

It is the *tragedy* that Christians should know about and pray about and care. The tragedy of childlessness, adultery, separation, promiscuity. Both in this town and also in our home town last year there were four unwed mothers aged 15 and nine were aged 16. In Washington, D.C., for example, more than 1100 girls under 18 had illegitimate babies last year. Hundreds of unhappy girls are leaping from girlhood to motherhood without experiencing the happy, carefree years of the average teenager. From this aspect alone the situation of these girls is tragic. The answer to the problem is a return to Christian standards of chastity and the sacredness of marriage. Wise words. But words the progressives will scoff at. Their stock replies "Old-fashioned" and "naïve". This is the real tragedy of the situation—that so many accept the words of the short-sighted thinkers. They should ask themselves whether any other code can really replace the "old-fashioned" standards. The "new freedom" for the young sounds all right in theory. The trouble is that in so many families it must be paid for with unhappiness and ruined lives.

LONELINESS

We rate loneliness a bigger problem than sex. For one thing it involves so many people : 6 million Britons live alone. Widows, spinsters and divorcees are the largest groups living alone. It is only too apparent that isolation and loneliness are the main factors that make for suicide. Much has been done already but only the fringe of this problem has been touched so far. The searchlight of publicity has revealed new areas of isolation and given new emphasis to others, such as weekend loneliness, loneliness on retirement, the loneliness of those tied to the home, of the 30 to 50 age group, of wives who are left alone when their husbands are working away from home or in the forces and in increasing measure, the loneliness of children under five.

It seems that we have learned how to make nuclear weapons, how to fly supersonic aircraft and how to build skyscrapers, yet we still do not know how to deal with one of the main social diseases of our time, loneliness. What are the causes of loneliness? One is the impersonality of town life, which is greatly intensified in this country by our passionate belief in "keeping oneself to oneself". We know instances on this housing estate of families who live in semi-detached houses and who have deliberately not spoken to the folk next door for years. If this is true of "veteran" inhabitants, it is increasingly difficult for newcomers who have to move when their industry moves. During 1960–63 we lived in a down-town industrial area near here where it was exceptional to have a front garden or a bathroom. Now most of that parish has been demolished and is being cleared in preparation for skyscraper flats. People have been compelled to uproot and make way for progress. Unfortunately there is no sign yet that loneliness on housing estates is only temporary and that estates speedily become neighbourhood units. When families on this estate go away for their summer holidays, the "neighbours" often steal all their fruit, vegetables and flowers. And children here are bored stiff after the first week of every holiday because there is nothing to do.

There are other trends in our modern society that make for loneliness. The decrease in the size of families during the last 50 years means fewer relations and far less natural social intercourse. One consequence of this may be that when a marriage is broken by death the remaining partner can be left very lonely, especially when there are no close relatives. Again, the great increase in divorces means more broken homes and possible loneliness for at least one of the partners. Again, the loss of religious beliefs during the past 50 years has contributed to the sense of loneliness felt by many, and the consequent decline in churchgoing has meant the loss to them of an opportunity for corporate worship and fellowship in a community of like-minded people. We would not press this decline because we have just conducted an exhaustive survey of this estate. This surprised us by revealing that four churches here are in definite contact with 1750 out of 3191 homes, well over half the families on the estate. (We now have four teams of 12 visiting the 1441 homes of "outsiders".)

A frequent cause of loneliness among middle-aged single folk is their lack of training in early life for any skilled occupation. This keeps them tied to unskilled, poorly paid and often boring jobs which leave them little time or energy to make new contacts or to take part in any social activity. For example, fewer watch football these days. This is partly due to expense. It now costs 5s. here just to stand and watch second division football of a very average quality. Another potential cause of loneliness may be a rise of the family or individual in the social scale. People lose contact with their original group and are sometimes unable to acclimatise themselves to the new. This cause may not be widespread because many families prefer to continue living in their council house even when the weekly income is £40–£50. There is perhaps less social entertaining these days and this increases loneliness. Reasons for this may be small houses, lack of domestic help, too much ready-made entertainment, too much pledged in hire-purchase.

Life in a bed-sitter can be very depressing. A survey in 1964 estimated that Britain has a population of 500,000 living in bed-sitting rooms. Apparently they pay £108 million a year in rent, another £12 million for heating and cooking and £125 million on food. Their favourite dish is sausages, consuming $1\frac{1}{2}$ million a week. They buy 750,000 tins of baked beans a week. *The majority eat, cook, sleep and wash in the same room, spending an average of 11 hours a day in it.* They borrow 95,000 books a week from public libraries. The average bed-sitter tenant moves to fresh digs once in three to four months. Women outnumber men by two to one. Many professional workers, too busy during the week to make outside contacts, find themselves at the week-end without a soul to speak to. "After the boss lets us out on Friday and the landlady has had her money on Saturday, only the grave-like silence of Sunday has to be endured before Monday comes again."

There can be real loneliness among children before they reach school age and this may affect their capacity for fitting into life in later years. Today's families are often small and spaced so that a child may have no companion of his own with whom to play. The only child is often a lonely child. Life in large blocks of flats is particularly hard on young children. There is rarely any adequate place for them to play, and many mothers are too busy to take a child out except when they go shopping, so the child gets no play with other children. Estates like ours are basically spacious and well planned but it is difficult for little children to meet each other in play because there is a lack of small playgrounds near the houses. There is an excellent mother and baby club which meets weekly in the church hall, but more foresight for children's needs is required when planning estates of 12,000–15,000 because thousands of the residents are under five. Children can be very lonely after school when they return hungry to empty houses, especially in the winter when it is cold and dark. There does not seem to be any economic reason for mothers who live in subsidised council houses to be out working when their children need them at home. There is an American extension to this problem. Five million U.S. families, or one in 10, are led by a woman, who invariably has to go out to work. One reason for this is that many of the 3 million divorced or separated women refuse alimony to show that they can be two parents in one. It seems urgent and obvious that we should not allow the feeling of isolation to develop among young children. How happily a person gets along as an adult in his job, in his family and social life, depends a great deal on how he got along with other children when he was young. The years of education are of vital importance because much loneliness can be traced to lack of outside interests as well as of inner resources of mind and spirit.

I

8

BLESSED ARE THE AFFLUENT?

So far we have looked at some of the problems connected with prosperity rather than poverty. Christians need to remind themselves that better wages, better housing, better medical care, better savings, better holidays, better education, have not produced paradise in Britain, the United States, or elsewhere. Indeed many who look closely at the problems on either side of the Atlantic are convinced that the affluent society is still a long way off. Certainly hardship exists today: it has not been abolished in either country. And hardship is not just suicide and sex, but hard conditions in daily life. Thus we must continue to probe some of the signs of the poverty of the sixties.

CONGESTION

We all know about crowded roads: do we also realise our country is choking? Before we discuss housing we must examine the prior question of our congested little island. The land problem is the problem of a rising birth rate in a small island—of 47 million people (54 million by 1981 and 64 million by 2000) living on only 37 million acres of dry land in England and Wales. Beyond this, however, the main shortages occur because the population is ill-distributed: 25 per cent of it lives in London, Birmingham and Manchester, and half of the population increase of the next 20 years will have to be absorbed by the south-east corner of the country. The British Governments over the next 20 years are faced with the problem of finding about 40,000 acres of farmland each year to turn over to urban development. Just how congested we are may be seen by a look at world density figures. The density of population in England and Wales, estimated at 790 per square mile in the 1961 census, is exceeded in Europe only by the Netherlands with 893. India, China and Japan, countries normally accounted over-populated, have a density of 642, 313 and 156 respectively. In the United States population per square mile averages 49.

It is this congestion in Britain, not speculation, which is push-
ing up land values. Speculators are thriving because of land
shortage; they are not by themselves the cause of high prices.
The Land Commission, by itself, will not resolve present difficulties; it cannot reduce the "natural" pressures which are affecting land values. Only cessation of population growth can achieve
this. In any case, it is probable that too much emphasis is being
put on the price of land. This is one commodity which cannot
be increased and is bound to get dearer as time goes on as it has
in other countries. When a piece of ground is purchased for
building, even at the rate of £10,000 per acre, this is only £2
per square yard, which is much less than a good carpet, or even
lino for that matter.

The population expansion was unexpected. Before the war
demographers anticipated that the population of Britain would
be down to 4 million by the twenty-first century—what it was in
the reign of Elizabeth I. Social scientists talked of a decadent
nation. Despite post-war increase, which produced a record total
881,000 births in 1947, the Royal Commission on population
visualised a continuing decline. In 1955 births dropped to
667,000. But this trend was reversed in the latter half of the
1950s. On the basis of present trends, the Registrar-General predicted that the birth-rate for 1965 will equal the predicted birth
rate for 1975 and that the population of England and Wales will
be 54 million by 1981, not the 47 million forecast only eight
years ago. But it looks as though officialdom and the computers
will be wrong again : the provisional figures for 1965 show a
"sizeable" fall, in the birth rate, for the first time in 10 years.

What appears to be a highly significant variation in the
American population pattern is disclosed by Government statistics on the birth rate. During 1965 it dropped to 100.5 live births
for each 1000 women of child-bearing age, compared with 122.7
eight years ago. Ever since 1958 there has been a gradual decline
in spite of the rising number of marriages and the increasing
number of women of child-bearing age. The births in 1965 fell
below 4 million for the first time since 1953, and population
growth is the smallest on a percentage basis since 1945.

This fundamental change is explained in a number of ways

and is upsetting a good many calculations about American society in the next few decades. The trend to large families which set in after the 1939–45 war has obviously been reversed, possibly because people in the middle classes are discovering what a heavy financial burden the education of their children is becoming as more and more of them want to go to college. At the same time the increasing use of birth control pills and other contraceptive devices is making it easier to regulate the size of families. The average marriage age has also been creeping upwards. It was 23.1 for men getting married for the first time last year, the highest since 1948, and 20.5 for women, the highest since 1947. Less housing and fewer schools and colleges may be needed, and plans for expansion in these fields may have to be curtailed. And as most babies are apparently coming from the people least able to afford them, it looks as though the campaign to abolish poverty will have to be pursued with increasing vigour and at an increasing cost.

The fact that these forecasts have been wrong means that social and economic problems—housing, immigration, education, urban development, health, transport, all spheres in which planning is influenced by the size of population—have been aggravated by the unexpected increased population. The acute shortage of beds in maternity hospitals is one of its most obvious results. The housing shortage has also been exacerbated. Post-war policy was based on the assumption that the population would remain stable, and was therefore concerned with providing housing for the overspill, estimated in 1956 to be 2 million people. This picture has now been dramatically transformed. In addition to coping with overspill and keeping pace with absolescence, we shall now have to find houses for 17 million more people in this century. But the really disturbing aspect of a high birth rate is the increase in the proportion of the dependent and unproductive to the working population: in the next dozen years the working population is expected to have risen by 2.55 million, compared with a predicted increase in the dependent population of 5.44 million. Not only is such an increase in itself undesirable, but it also involves heavy capital expenditure on health, education and social welfare services and absorbs a disproportionate number of highly skilled personnel. But even if domestic planning and our economic resources can cope with the situation, geographical factors make the increase alarming. As the population expands, open countryside shrinks and congestion chokes our cities.

HOUSING

Although housing conditions are improving gradually, there is no doubt about hardship; thousands of families still live in very primitive homes. The latest Housing Tables published by the Stationery Office indicate that at least $1\frac{1}{2}$ million households (11–12 per cent) have no inside lavatory. This causes great inconvenience for very young children, the sick and elderly. There are nearly another million households (5.8 per cent) which have only a shared use of a lavatory. Households entirely without a fixed bath numbered 3.64 million, 22 per cent as compared with 37 per cent 10 years ago. Households sharing a fixed bath numbered 670,990 (46 per cent). According to the Statistical Office of the European Communities, 73 per cent of homes in the United Kingdom have bathrooms, compared with 61 per cent in Sweden, 49 per cent in West Germany, 28 per cent in France and 13 per cent in Italy.

Over three million families (20 per cent) in Britain in 1965 have no hot water tap. Families lacking even a cold water tap numbered 246,000 (1.7 per cent) compared with 6 per cent 10 years ago and families sharing a cold water tap numbered 310,000. This is supposed to be the press-button age; the era of automation, space travel and atomic energy. But the affluent society has a long way to go. Progress is slow, but gradually more homes are being modernised. In the past five years in England and Wales alone more than 153,000 homes have been equipped with a bath or shower, over 243,000 have been supplied with hot water and over 148,000 have had indoor lavatories, all installed with standard grants for basic amenities. At the time of the last census (1961) about a quarter of all households had one room or less available for living, eating or sleeping for each member of the household, compared with a third in 1951. Household sizes differ noticeably for tenure groups. The average household consists of three people, but local authority tenants have 3.6, and private tenants 2.6.

The problem of homelessness is acute not only in London or Glasgow, but in all parts of the country. It should be the duty of every congregation to look around its parish, discover the families in need and then study its latent resources to see whether it can afford to establish its own housing society in order to help them. Four Church leaders in Scotland have urged a national effort to remove "the most urgent problem in this land today". In Scotland today there are about 490,000 pre-1860 houses and 550,000 pre-1880, and the improvement rate, in spite of increased legislation, is minimal. In Glasgow there are 80,000 persons on the waiting list for municipal houses, 34,000 live more than four to a room, and 890,000 more than three to a room. Last Christmastide there were at least 100,000 men and women homeless and destitute throughout Britain. Already this situation is deteriorating. So far the Welfare State has proved ineffectual in dealing with the thousands who inhabit reception centres, common lodging houses, hostels, bombed and derelict buildings, public gardens and parks and railway stations. Many discharged ex-mental patients are wandering around the country and about 2000 men and women will be "sleeping rough" in London tonight.

OLD AGE

We are getting older! As a result senior citizens form an increasing proportion of the Western world. In 1901 the number of people in Britain over 60 was about 2.4 million. By 1921 that had risen to 3.6 million. By 1941 it was 5.9 million, an increase of 3.5 million in 40 years—and it is continuing to grow. This is far in excess of the rise in the total population. By 1961 the total had reached 8 million over 60, and by 1970 it will be almost 10 million: soon one person in six will be over 65.

A great deal of nonsense is often talked about our affluent society. "For some millions of elderly people it means a life of biting poverty," says one of our M.P.s. But fortunately there is another side to this picture. The position of old people today may be one of our blind-spots. The elderly are very well cared for in this town; one local ward, for example, distributed £6500 to pensioners last Christmas. On this housing estate we have two modern old folk's homes, and two more within a mile of the parish, and there are several groups of small bungalows reserved for individual elderly folk and well situated near shops, buses and other houses. In the past week we have tried here and in our previous down-town industrial parish to find a pensioner who would like a radio set ready-licensed; countless enquiries were made to find someone in need (most of the old folk have T.V.). The only cause of hardship is that in 1963 this estate became a smokeless zone and this compels us to buy expensive smokeless fuel, costing much more than coal. But this is typical of a problem which affects the *whole* community. It is true that pensioners found most of the 12s. 6d. rise in March, 1965 to be absorbed in rising prices: but some sections of the community did not even have that rise. There are many *young* families who would like an extra 12s. 6d. every week to offset the rise in prices.

A great deal is being done for the elderly, much more than was ever done by them for their parents and grandparents. We probably visit more pensioners than any other age group— either living alone, or with their children, or old folk's homes or in hospital. The elderly are not beyond the reach of the affluent society: many are living very happily and comfortably and very few have *only* the state pension to support them. Four times as many bedridden old people live with relatives as in institutions. Care of senior citizens is a sphere in which we are much concerned and occasionally we are challenged by those who say that there is real poverty today in this and every town. We always say to these critics that we are free at any time of the day for them to show us this "real poverty" but without success. We ourselves have never come across pensioners sitting huddled in overcoats in front of empty grates. Before Father Joe Williamson retired from his parish in Stepney, in London's tough East End, we frequently helped him and saw poor housing at first hand. We thought perhaps we had "blinkers" on until we met a Salvation Army brigadier who was working full time in that London East End district. When we asked him how many cases of real hardship he had met he said *"Only one in three years"*.

During the period 1948–65 there has been an increase of 217 per cent in the pension rate for single people and 214 per cent for married couples. These increases should be considered against an increase of 80 per cent in the index of retail prices, 106 per cent in the index of wages rates and 163 per cent in the average earnings of adult manual workers. These figures are the latest available in 1965 from the Ministry of Pensions and National Insurance.

Appearances can deceive. Those who seem to be rich are not always wealthy, and vice versa. Folk can and do have modest tastes or an austere home and yet have plenty of money. People do not always refrain from drinking or smoking or T.V. simply because of cost. Those who seem "poor old pensioners" or "poor patients" in hospitals or special homes are sometimes quite wealthy. Recently we officiated at a wedding where a retiring collection was announced. The bride's grandfather was there, dressed very modestly as usual. When he approached the plate, he pulled out a handful of silver. When he could not find a sixpence, he put all the half-crowns and florins back saying to the verger, "I haven't any change". We might have been very sympathetic and not expected an old man to be able to afford more than sixpence even at his grand-daughter's wedding : presumably he only has his pension to live on : He died recently— *and left over £150,000 net.*

Nevertheless there is a real social problem. The elderly have been hit by rising food and fuel bills. Some old folk must be suffering real hardship and loneliness. It is good that pension and National Assistance rates are constantly being increased to match the retail price index. National Assistance is received by 21 per cent of people over retirement age. A recent survey indicated that there may be thousands of old people in Britain living near the poverty line set by National Assistance standards. They must be found by Christians. And we must look after our own elderly relations and friends, and also save for our own old age so that we are not a problem for the community. Certainly at the rate that the people of this country are saving money, there should be no problems of hardship for tomorrow's veterans : but of course it depends on what we mean by "hardship".

IMMIGRATION

Perhaps the section of Britain which suffers most today are the coloured folk. Certainly they constitute one of the most difficult problems of the Welfare State. One of the "signs" of the times is that we are becoming a coloured community. According to the latest estimates for mid-65 the total number of coloured immigrants living in Britain is now well over 1 million. Despite the Commonwealth Immigration Act, which restricted entry, the number of new immigrants continues to rise, thousands by illegal entry. Most immigrants come from the West Indies, India and Pakistan. Experts predict that coloured families here will produce a million babies by 1980 and that this will then give a coloured population of some 3 million. Whatever our views and prejudices we have to accept the fact that we *are* a mixed-race nation.

Proper control of immigration has now been conceded even by the Labour Party, but what is to be done about the immigrants already established here and especially about their children? It is expected that in one town not far from here one-fifth of the children in secondary modern schools will be coloured by 1968. In another area it has been calculated that this year the proportion of school-leaving immigrants will be 3 per cent and that in 10 years' time it will be 15 per cent. In another northern city the council decided that from September, 1965 the proportion of immigrants in any one of its 120 primary schools is to be limited to 25 per cent. The number in the classroom is restricted to 30 per cent or 15 per cent if they are non-English speaking. Before the new plan was approved one school had more than 50 per cent immigrants. It is useless to deny that this constitutes a problem and equally useless to suggest that the problem will solve itself if it is tacitly ignored. When youth employment officers state that they spend as much time placing immigrant school-leavers in suitable posts as they do searching for suitable jobs for handicapped children, the time has come for serious reconsideration.

The Minister of Labour has already taken action. He is prepared to withdraw employment exchange facilities from any employer who shows continued resistance to taking on coloured

people. This is just and right. But is the employer always to
blame? May he not have to consider prejudice among his existing workers or among his clients or customers? It is altogether
too easy to demand a stand for right and justice when those
who demand it have nothing to lose, while those from whom
it is demanded risk trouble and loss. It is, again, too facile to
suggest that race-prejudice is un-Christian and immoral. Of
course it is. But it will not be eradicated until its implications are
faced, and until it is generally understood that the assimilation
of minorities has, throughout history, presented grave difficulties.
Racial relationships are essentially personal and all branches of
the community have a national duty to accept their responsibilities. A wise bishop sent out a pastoral letter last Lent
which included these words "We must rid our hearts utterly of
anything proud or patronising or condescending in our relation
with our fellow-men of other races. This mental respect for one
another is what is meant when we speak of mutual responsibility
within the body of Christ."

Foreign students number about one in 10 at British universities and this proportion is slowly rising. Countries from which
the largest number of full-time students came last year were:

India	1746	Canada	652	S. Africa	423
U.S.A.	1295	Iraq	530	Australia	414
Nigeria	1090	Malaysia	481	Kenya	393
Pakistan	749	Egypt	452	Ghana	301

Of the students enrolled in 1964–65 8280 came from other
parts of the Commonwealth and 5837 from non-Commonwealth
countries. The main subjects being studied are: Arts, 3310;
technology, 3269; social studies, 2574; pure science, 2448;
medicine 1965. Thus the number of overseas university students
here is about 15,000, almost equivalent to the number of British
undergraduates at Oxford and Cambridge combined. In addition there are about 48,300 overseas students in our technical
colleges and other non-university institutions, following full-time
courses of study. In some London technical colleges more than
half the students are coloured. Overseas students form 32 per

cent of the entire post-graduate student body in Britain. Commonwealth students attending British educational institutions cost about £8 million out of public funds and the Government spends a further £16 million a year on educational aid to developing countries, of which about 80 per cent goes to the Commonwealth. This large number of overseas students creates problems for the authorities in the universities and research centres, and more and more specific courses are being organised to accommodate these students, whose needs differ substantially from those of domestic ones. If the African student, for example, absorbs what he sees and hears in Britain or Russia or the United States, he will return home only to find that he has lost contact with his own society. The result is very often that the student abroad is really not at home anywhere. He is attracted and repelled at the same time by both Britain and Africa. No wonder that many a young intellectual has returned home a revolutionary, rebelling against both past and present.

Of course the reverse may be true. African countries which have become independent recently are having difficulty in recalling their students from courses abroad. This is becoming an acute problem and Nigeria, Ghana and Kenya, for example, are becoming increasingly aware of the lack of trained brain-power necessary to carry on administration effectively. Students who have gone abroad for training are hesitating to return, either because they have found more remunerative jobs in Britain or because they are out of sympathy with their government. Even in their own countries advanced education may be a liability as well as an asset because opportunities for suitable employment are not always available. In India today, for instance, there are about 2 million unemployed high school graduates and a further 200,000 unemployed who are proud possessors of a B.A. The Philippines have about 100,000 unemployed college graduates. These are people who have been awakened to a new sense of human dignity. But where are bread and freedom?

It might be thought that the problem of too many immigrants has an important bearing on overcrowding and population density. Obviously this must be true to some extent but it is more than balanced by the number of *emigrants*. The total number emigrating last year went up from 127,000 in 1963 to 170,000 last year, a rise of 33 per cent. The number who went to the main receiving countries of the Commonwealth, Canada, Australia, New Zealand and the Rhodesian Federation increased from 77,524 to 105,651. Other Commonwealth countries took 26,000 and thousands went to the United States. There were 46,989 departures from Britain during last year under the assisted passage scheme to Australia. This was 17,738 more than in 1963. Preliminary estimates for 1966–67 indicate that the number of emigrants may exceed the immigrants. Hardly a ship or plane now leaves this country without taking with it a drop of the rich red life-blood of this country—doctors, scientists, teachers, engineers, nurses—our best men and women trained at the expense of the taxpayers. The 1965 flood has been on such a scale that it has been the means of setting up lucrative businesses which sell British brains abroad in return for handsome commissions.

REDUNDANCY

This could be *the* problem of the next 10 years. It is political, economic and social in implication, and it can have a severity which clergy and others in positions of security cannot easily appreciate. Certainly redundancy (with integration) has been the top social-economic problem in the States throughout the sixties and one which we shall have to face increasingly in Britain in the seventies. America is the wealthiest country in the world with the highest standards of living and Americans have worked very hard to bring this about, aided by their good fortune in not being invaded or bombed in World War Two. But even America has a serious balance of payments deficit, similar to that in Britain. At the beginning of this year the deficit was about £1250 million. This is caused by military spending overseas (defence spending is about half the U.S. budget of £35,700 million). Foreign aid programmes (at £1200 million, the smallest since Marshall aid began), tourism and heavy American investment in Britain and Europe. (We all know American Fords of Dagenham but there are many others like Gillette and Woolworths, and one person in five in Southampton today is employed by America.)

But even in this land of freedom, of progress and prosperity, *there is poverty*. And much of it is caused by progress. This sounds absurd. But this is precisely what is happening through automation. Precise estimates vary but automation is gobbling up jobs at the rate of 40,000 to 70,000 a week. This means that between 2 million and $3\frac{1}{2}$ million men are being thrown out of work every year in a country where there are already 4 million unemployed. Unless this problem is tackled urgently and immediately there will be 10–12 million jobless in the United States in three or four years' time. Some union leaders think that this total may rise as high as 15 million—a terrifying millstone of unemployment that could well bring the American economy to a complete and disastrous halt.

President Johnson is giving a vigorous lead. In his inaugural speech on 20th January, 1965, he declared "In a land of great wealth, families must not live in hopeless poverty. In a land rich in harvest, children must not go hungry. In a land of healing miracles, neighbours must not suffer and die untended. In a land of learning, young people must be taught to read and write." And he sent to Congress a Budget for 1965–66 which asked for a large increase to £400 million for health social welfare services, education, housing and "war on poverty".

This is the heart of the dilemma, this is a Christian matter: namely that in the affluence of 1965 both the American President and our own Prime Minister should be publicly dedicating themselves to the abolition of *poverty*. Yet, in fact, according to official figures somewhere between 30 million and 40 million— roughly 20 per cent of the total population, and the majority of them *white*—are living in poverty and squalor in slums, migratory labour camps, depressed areas or Indian reservations; all below the minimum accepted standards of health, housing and education. Yes, at least 30 million people go hungry . . . in 1965 . . . not in India or the Far East or any of the deprived African nations . . . *but in America.*

What is happening over there? Only seven years ago there were only 450 computers in America; today there are 18,000 and this figure may be doubled by 1967–68. The "miracles" that these electronic brains perform with such bewildering speed and uncanny accuracy are even more astonishing than the factory robots. In Michigan, for example, a utility company supplying electricity to 50,000 homes has fired 300 meter-readers and half the office staff. Customers are now linked to a computer that registers the current consumed, reckons the monthly accounts and even addresses them. Another of these extraordinary machines can work out in less than half an hour the payroll for a factory of 26,000 employees—taking into account varying hourly rates, overtime and tax deductions. There is another machine that can print a 300-page book in three hours—a job that would take a printer a month to complete, working 12 hours a day six days a week.

This is only the beginning. Wait till the seventies. Even more fantastic developments are ahead, with machines capable of drawing blue-prints and making medical diagnoses. This is the shape of things to come and it should, of course, herald an era of unequalled prosperity and wealth. But the giant robots that line the horizon of America's automated future are already casting dark and menacing shadows. Instead of serving mankind, these machines may blow world economy sky high and bring widespread poverty, misery and unemployment. Already there have been serious declines in the labour forces of many American industries. We ourselves have visited some of these depressed mining and steel areas, where 16 per cent are unemployed. Automation has taken the jobs of 400,000 coal miners since the war. In the same period 250,000 steel workers have been replaced by machines and 300,000 textile workers have lost their jobs.

White collar workers, too, are being pushed out by sophisticated computers. One U.S. Government department, for example, handling veterans' pensions, has cut its staff from 17,000 to 3000 since installing electronic equipment. There is a radio factory in Chicago with a line of clicking, purring, winding robots producing 1000 transistor sets a day—tended by only *two men*. A year ago 200 men were employed on the same job. In New York there is a bottling plant where 200,000 bottles a day are washed, refilled, capped and crated. Total staff—three men! The New York telephone exchange is 20 storeys high and handles millions of calls every day. And is operated by a staff of five, two on duty and three on stand-by. We ourselves found that by dialling 14 digits we could connect with almost anyone in the States within a few seconds. And Macey's, the world-famous New York store, has been experimenting with a robot salesgirl that sells 36 different garments in 10 styles and sizes, accepts either coin or notes, gives correct change—and rejects, with a suitably indignant scream, all counterfeit money.

America is facing mounting competition in international markets and has its own balance-of-payments problems and cannot lag behind in the automation race. She must produce more and more goods at lower and lower costs. Automation is the only answer and its progress cannot be halted. George Meany, president of the A.F.L.–C.I.O. (American Federation of Labour–Congress of Industrial Relations), America's T.U.C., says, "There is no element of blessing in automation. It is rapidly becoming a real curse to society and it could bring us to a national catastrophe." But there is general agreement among industrialists and trade union leaders alike, that in a competitive world industry must adopt the most modern and streamlined techniques to survive. No one had yet come up with a complete answer. Earlier retirement (55 is suggested) and longer holidays (already 10 weeks for some) are all high in labour's programme to combat the robots. In the car industry they are talking of "phased retirement" through which a man would be working only six months a year by the time he reaches 60. *What happens when man is unnecessary?*

Pay people a full week's wages for staying at home and *not* working. This is the startling plan put before President Johnson by a group of 32 economists and scientists. They believe that men will have to be paid for not working because automation, within a few decades, will mean that nine out of 10 jobs in the U.S. will be done by machine. They have suggested a minimum "wage" of 100 dollars (£35) a week for a non-working married man with one child, with higher rates for larger families. "Society must accept that work as we know it must eventually disappear. Man, as a working instrument, is heading towards obsolescence." Women, likewise, it seems; a machine is being tested which is likely to render the human cook obsolete for certain dishes. Without human help, it can mass-produce for restaurants hamburgers, fried chicken, chips, fried shrimps, frankfurters and milk shakes. And in Sweden a computer has just chosen a beauty queen! Instead of employing a panel of judges the organisers of the "Queen of Gothenburg" contest hired a computer and fed it with the vital statistics of the hundreds of entrants.

Will America become the master—or the victim—of automation? At heart this is a *theological* question. Extravagant hopes and exaggerated fears have been aroused by the first large-scale introduction of giant computers and new fully-automated equipment, even though vast stretches of the economy have yet to see their first computer. Until a few months ago automation was under a thick black cloud, the whipping-boy for the national concern felt by the stubbornly-irreducible core of American unemployment which runs into millions. The concern is understandable. From down-town Los Angeles to up-town New York, from the rural slums of the South to the displaced workers of Northern industrial cities, poverty is encountered to a degree almost unknown in post-war Britain. Geographically widespread, unemployment is also dangerously concentrated among the unskilled, uneducated and coloured. It builds up in a series of unfavourable combinations to a frightening 30 per cent rate among female Negro teenagers. In these conditions anything appearing to intensify the problem comes under suspicion.

In the mid-nineteen-sixties the American Government, like the British, has been desperately trying to encourage modernisation in industry. It was the computer's particular misfortune that it came into public consciousness at a time when, for quite different reasons, the U.S. economy was suffering from a slow rate of growth and from high unemployment. In 1966–67 the great debate on automation is entering a new phase. Its tone has been set by the emphatic text laid down by the Secretary of Labour: "Automation creates more jobs than it destroys". The good as well as the bad which computers may bring is most clearly foreshadowed by a recent report of the 500 top industrial companies, among which undoubtedly are to be found the pace-

setters in automation. These industrial giants since 1959 . . .
jumped their investment in property, plant and equipment by
59 per cent, more than twice the rate of their smaller competitors. (For perspective in 1956 the giants had only £4500 invested
per employee, but since then it has taken more than £24,000 in
investment to support each new job.) . . . boosted sales by
33 per cent, roughly three times the rate of sales gains among
small firms . . . created 11 per cent more new jobs, while the
number of persons employed by the rest of U.S. industry actually
declined.

Clearly the new technology is benefiting the leading industrial
corporations and helping them grow even faster. Computers are
suggesting designs for cars, translating books, helping to design
other computers, teaching mathematics, landing aircraft and
diagnosing diseases. Doctors, school-teachers, professional engineers and newspapermen are among many varied occupations
now being relieved of part of their work and freed to develop the
less routine aspects.

But will all these gains have to be paid for by even greater
hardship among other sections of the community? Automation
is only one, though admittedly the most spectacular of the forces
which are reshaping the industrial scene on both sides of the
Atlantic. New materials and processes are obsoleting entire
industries, new industrial and commercial centres are gaining
prominence at the direct expense of old competitors, new jobs
are springing up while many traditional skills go begging and
unemployment remains high. Perhaps the most perplexing problem is the concentration of industrial power in the hands of
relatively few mammoth corporations. We seem to be passing
from the era of the too-powerful union to the era of the too-
powerful company. The 20 largest manufacturing companies
control a quarter of America's industrial capacity. About 75 per
cent of manufacturing assets are in the hands of 1000 companies.
This means that the assets of the top 20 are virtually equal to
those of the remaining 419,000 firms. A handful of firms can
now dominate a whole industry : for instance, four manufacturers
control 80 per cent of all car, 70 per cent of all tobacco and
50 per cent of all dairy product sales.

K

The power of the giants has been growing quietly during the past few years, and America is just beginning to notice that by 1970 200 corporations may control the country's economy. In the long run there is no economic alternative to increasing efficiency, improving quality and providing completely new services. When, in addition, computers present government and industry with greater powers for ironing-out fluctuations—by more up-to-date information on economic trends, better control over stocks, more accurate predictions—the chances are of more, not less, employment. Given comprehensive retraining facilities and social benefits, automation is to be welcomed, especially for a country like Britain.

People matter more than machines

This situation is of great concern to the homes of families on both sides of the Atlantic. Already automation has claimed millions of "victims". *The more progress, the more hardship and poverty.* And Christians are being involved whether we like it or not. Britain is poised on the threshold of this fascinating and frightening new world of automation and redundancy. Are we likely to face the same grim problems that are causing such grave concern in the United States? Most American experts think that this is unlikely because automation, although inevitable, will not make any serious impact on the labour market here for at least two or three years. This will give us vital time to plan and "cushion" against the shock.

But we must awake: automation is coming to Britain fast. A typical example in autumn 1965 is the electronically-powered signal box being developed by British Rail. As a result of this modernisation, trains from London to Manchester are now controlled by only 11 signal boxes. And the electronically-powered box near here, for instance, now controls 159 track miles and has replaced 22 ordinary signal boxes, making a saving of 60 staff previously involved in controlling trains.

Time is on our side at the moment; time for planning, not for complacency. The report published this month by the Manpower Research Unit states that automation will have no significant effect on unemployment in the next five years. This is very optimistic, judging from American experience. Apparently we should be worrying instead about the manpower shortage which shows signs of causing serious production bottlenecks in the immediate future. This first report makes two points of considerable importance. The first is that the working population is expected to increase much more slowly than the total population during the next decade. The ratio to those who are economically dependent will therefore decrease. At present there are only three workers to one pensioner. The second point, based on the assumption of a continued high level of economic activity, is that there will be "at least sufficient jobs in total for the additional workers foreseen". Patterns of employment will certainly change markedly in Britain in 1967–70; but the main task, it seems, will still be to find and train the people to fill the jobs.

The conclusion to which these projections point is sternly simple. There must be far more efficient and flexible use of the labour force in the coming years. This is hardly the first time such a view has been put forward. But automation brings it to a head: we can either deploy our manpower or look forward to mass unemployment on the American scale. This question of deployment is crucial. When we talk of unemployment, we tend to overlook *unfilled vacancies*. At the beginning of 1966 there were 339,000 unemployed in Britain; at the same time there were 373,000 unfilled vacancies. The coming of automation makes it the more urgent that all co-operate to deploy and take up these vacancies. By 1967–68 we shall no longer be able to tolerate a situation in which labour restrictions, low-class management, inadequate redundancy provision and insufficient retraining facilities combine to foster waste and inefficiency in the deployment of British manpower. In all these areas a start towards reform has been made. Management training is being improved. Industrial training boards are being set up. The development of a national redundancy scheme is being discussed. But the Government can go only so far. Beyond a certain point the choice between a more or a less productive use of the country's resources depends on managements and, even more, on the unions.

The main reason for our present immunity from automation

unemployment is that labour relations have so far been handled with care and forethought. When new machines are being installed, drastic reductions in labour are made by "natural wastage" rather than large-scale sackings. We are able to learn from America and this has made some adjustments easier and more acceptable. Typical is the electric plant installed by a Yorkshire steel firm over more than two years, cutting the labour force of 2000 by half. Men have been retired or left, but not one has been dismissed. British Rail has made a reduction of 18,000 men—31 per cent of those employed in the main railway workshops—and this has been carried out smoothly and with the minimum of hardship over the last two years. The only serious problem was the re-employment of men over 60. There is a natural tendency to assume that redundancy is limited to the lower levels in industry, and that our sympathy and compensation be directed almost exclusively to such workers. But takeovers, to quote one example, generally cause more redundancy in management than lower down the line. Some 2000 company chiefs, experienced men in their fifties, are declared redundant each year.

There seems every reason to hope that no great hardship need be caused to the men involved in the reduction of any industry's labour force if it is done properly. There are at least five conditions necessary to keep hardship and upheaval at the absolute minimum:

1. careful, long-term planning.
2. the longest and frankest possible warning of intention.
3. close collaboration with Ministries and local authorities.
4. a generous redundancy compensation scheme.
5. very careful and sympathetic management.

So firm is the conclusion that upheaval can in fact be kept to the absolute minimum that it is now beginning to be appreciated that fears of hardship associated with the transfer of labour should not be used as an argument for artificially supporting a diminishing industry at the expense of withholding labour from growth industries. Nevertheless the increasing problems of

automation and redundancy are imposing the gravest responsibility on management. We had a senior engineer in the aircraft
industry come and talk over this problem with us: there was
redundancy at the firm and he had to reduce his section by
20 per cent, which meant sacking three men. The last three men
to be employed all had special mitigating circumstances as to
why they should not be dismissed. The whole section knew that
the senior engineer had personally to decide which three to sack
and he had two weeks to make up his mind: the worry made
him ill. When he gave his decision to the management, *they told
him that they had already decided not to sack anyone.*

In the next three or four years we must learn how to take the
full impact of automation, which is still to come in Britain, and
also the full impact of international trading and competition
with other nations where automation is also increasing, and to
derive from it the greatest benefit for the greatest number. Pain-
fully we have to learn that the rest of the world does not owe
us a higher standard of living than our fellow-men enjoy elsewhere. If we want to maintain a high standard of living, we
have to earn it by selling to other nations goods which they want,
well made, delivered on time, and at prices which they are
prepared to pay; and we shall only achieve this if in all sections
of the community there is a new spirit of co-operation, of hard
work and of service. "The only thing that will solve Britain's
problems is the long overdue reawakening of the British people
. . . the greatest myth of all is that salvation can come out of
selfishness."

9

STARVATION BY 1980

PERHAPS the most bitter fact in the world is that it is divided between those with white skins in relatively rich countries and a much larger number of men who have coloured skins and who are desperately poor. The Christian Church is largely made up of white people in the rich countries. In the world today the gap between these groups is not growing smaller and in some respects it is clearly growing wider. The rich white "Christian" West is not as sensitive to this offence to God as the facts demand, while poor coloured countries suspect that the riches of the West have been increased by exploitation of themselves.

If we reduce all the peoples on the earth into an imaginary town of 1000 persons, in proportion to their relative numbers of interest, population and religions of the world, such a town would be made up like this:

> 330 people would be Christians.
> 100 people would be Protestants.
> 230 people would be Roman Catholics and Orthodox.
> 270 people would be of other religions.
> 697 persons would be coloured.
> 303 persons would be white.
> 250 persons would be Chinese.
> 80 persons would be Communists.
> 370 persons would be under Communist domination.
> 280 persons would be unable to read or write.

Half of the town would be entirely ignorant of Jesus Christ but more than half would be familiar with the teachings of Marx and Lenin. In this mythical town there would be 16 British and also 60 Americans, who would receive half the entire income of the town. The Americans would have 15 times as much wealth per person as the rest of the town. They would produce

16 per cent of the food supply. They would eat 72 per cent above the food requirements of the rest, but yet would eat most of what they produced or would store it away for themselves at great expense. Since the rest of the town would be hungry and thirsty a large part of the time, there would be considerable resentment against the Americans. And the Americans would be busy spending £300 a year on military expenses, but only 300 pennies to further their religious beliefs with the rest of the town.

This is one way to look at the world. And look we must, for Christ's sake. God so loves not this land, not Western civilisation, but the whole world. Taking a world view is admittedly difficult: we cannot escape prejudice and it is well nigh impossible to evaluate world statistics meaningfully. There is often a lack of reliable evidence and what information is available is difficult to verify. However it is possible to see some of the trends. For example, the Christians in Asia are estimated to be 3.2 per cent of a population of 1575.6 million. Even if both figures are subject to, say, 25 per cent error, they still demonstrate that Christians are a tiny minority on this vast continent. Or again, it is generally agreed that well-fed Western man eats about 10 times as much as an African on the bare subsistence level. Suppose in fact we are only eating five times as much as Africans, it still remains a fact that we are well-fed and they are not. Again, there are 140,000 more people in the world today than there were yesterday. This is the latest official revised estimate of the United Nations. Suppose the actual figure is 100,000 or 180,000: will the population problem vanish? Experts will still differ on whether the world can sustain its growing population in 20 or 30 years' time, and they will go on producing contradictory statistics to prove opposite conclusions.

As an approximate guide we may take it that at present 60 per cent of the world population lives on 7 per cent of the land area of this globe. The three main areas of dense population are respectively: the Asian Monsoon area—1100 million people on 2.4 million square miles; the temperate zone of Europe—400 million people on 1.2 million square miles; the Atlantic coast of North America—100 million people on 0.4

million square miles. One problem seems to be that there are in the foreseeable future no other areas where a similar concentration of people and economic resources seem in prospect. It is a well known fact that a large part of the world's surface is too dry or too cold for the cultivation of crops. At present roughly 10 per cent is under cultivation, 20 per cent is pasture land, 30 per cent is woodland or forest and 40 per cent is without agricultural value. An expansion of cropland at the expense of pasture and forest is possible and necessary if future populations are to be fed. Irrigation schemes are costly but they can reclaim at least a fraction of the world's desert and dams can provide electric power. We ourselves worked in Palestine for three months some years ago and were very impressed by desert irrigation schemes in progress. But the problem is there. Even the U.S.A. has increasing difficulties over soil erosion and timber shortage.

The world race of the sixties and seventies is not so much one between population and food supply, but a race between what can be done and what will be done. The Aswan Dam, for example, is increasing Egypt's cultivatable land by a third. But in the 15 years it has taken to complete, Egypt's population has already increased far more than a third. Progress cannot be even. Food production in the world has been increasing since 1948 at 2.7 per cent—almost twice as fast as population increase, which is now approaching 2 per cent. In the Far East over the last 10 years food production has increased by 3 per cent and the population by 1.4 per cent. p.a. The difficulty, however, is that some of the poorer countries are actually losing ground and are worse off economically today than they were in the mid-fifties. In spite of greater food production and increased imports, Asians generally had less to eat per person than before the 1939–45 war. The size of the world population is less of a food problem than its uneven distribution.

In the so-called developed countries—we are all developing nations really—and in particular the United States and Northern Europe, no shortage of calories on average exists. But two-thirds of the world's people live in countries with nutritionally inadequate national diets. The diet deficit areas include the whole of

Asia except Japan and Israel, all but the southern tip of Africa, the northern part of South America and the Caribbean. The diet of people in these areas averaged 900 calories per day below the level of the one-third of the world living in countries with adequate national average diets. The basic problem of the diet deficit countries is one of productivity. The people cannot produce enough food to feed themselves or produce enough other products to afford to buy the food they require. The daily calorie intake in the United States, Argentina, Britain, Scandinavia, and Australia is over 3000. Canada, the Soviet Union and Western Europe have between 2600 and 3000. Central America, Brazil, West and South Africa, Egypt and Central Europe have between 2200 and 2600. The rest, including most of Africa and all of Asia, have less than 2200.

This means that between 400 and 500 million people even in normal times do not get enough food of any description. Three-quarters of the world's children are growing up in these areas of almost entire want. In parts of West Africa 250 out of every 1000 children die before they are one year old (the rate in Britain is 22 per 1000) and the average Indian gets only 7lb. of meat or fish a year while people here can expect to eat 178lb. If people are not fully nourished they cannot generate either physical or mental energy. Without physical energy people cannot work properly even traditional methods; and without energy they cannot learn better methods whereby they may grow more nourishing crops at less expense to the soil. Apathy springs not so much from the acceptance of the will of Allah as from sheer exhaustion.

What makes the position frightening is the persistent weakness of commodity prices and the impact that this is having on the plans of developing countries. Cocoa provides an extreme though not an untypical example. The real worth of a ton of cocoa is now actually lower than in the depression years of the early thirties. Sugar prices have been falling steeply and stand below pre-war values in real terms. Coffee, tea and jute are all commodities where the long-term earnings outlook is poor.

For the countries who rely heavily on these commodity exports, this is a frightening position. Most are already poor.

Ghana has two-thirds of its export trade in cocoa; Mauritius virtually its entire export in sugar; as does Cuba; the Indians have one-third of their exports in tea and jute.

Another equally vexing problem is the shifting pattern of refugees. As the mass of fugitives from Eastern Europe has gradually been absorbed into the Western World, wave after wave of Africans have been driven from their homes by new political upheavals. At a rough estimate there are now about 400,000 refugees in Africa south of the Sahara. Fresh eruptions are possible at any moment in many potential trouble spots, including Rhodesia, South Africa and South-West Africa. The Portuguese territories have already disgorged many thousands of refugees and are the most likely scenes of disturbance in the near future. Here is a brief, limited list of some aspects of the world refugee problem :

1. 150,000 Tutsi tribesmen have fled Rwanda since independence brought the Hutu tribe to power.
2. There are still more than 1 million Arab refugees in Palestine.
3. Events in the Congo caused some 50,000 Congolese to seek refuge in neighbouring countries.
4. 280,000 refugees have entered India recently from East Pakistan.
5. Hongkong houses over a million Chinese refugees and Macao another 75,000.
6. There are some 35,000 Tibetan refugees in India and 8000 in Nepal.
7. Even in Europe, some 10,000 refugees from Communist States still arrive each year.

Nevertheless, in spite of these vast problems, some progress is expected during the rest of this decade. By 1970 the calories level in developing countries is expected to be 8 per cent above 1959–61 level. Consumption of protein and fat should be up 10 per cent and 16 per cent respectively. This indicates a marked improvement not only in the quantity of food per person but also an improvement in quality. Food production is mounting. The Commonwealth established a new record in the production of the main grains last year. The total was 130 million tons, forming 19 per cent of the world production. Commonwealth exports of grain at over 20 million tons were substantially higher than in 1963. Its share of the world trade rose from 22 per cent to 25 per cent. The output of rice in India and Pakistan reached a record of more than 47 million tons.. From the latest figures on food production it has been calculated that if all cultivable land was cultivated, the world would be capable of supporting a population of 28 billion—10 times its present figure—or 90 billion on a predominantly cereal diet. And there seems to be no danger of an exhaustion of fuel. Even if petroleum supplies were inadequate—improbable—it would be possible to produce sufficient motor fuel from coal, shale or compressed hydrogen. The estimated numbers of years' supply of minerals for a world population of 28 billion consuming at the same rate per head as the U.S. population in 1965 is:

Aluminium	3.1×10^7	Lead	1.2×10^5
Iron	5.0×10^6	Zinc	3.0×10^4
Copper	5.5×10^5	Tin	1.0×10^4

But fresh water is a problem. In both Britain and America water supplies are a serious national problem. We may not realise it but most of mankind is desperate for water. The lack of it is causing death and disease and thwarting economic development. Lack of rainfall is very serious. In some African countries 1965 was the third or fourth consecutive year without normal rainfall. This means . . . seeds fail to germinate . . . crops wither . . . pasture dries up . . . almost 100 per cent failure of harvest in some parts . . . cattle deaths up to 50 per cent . . . oxen too weak to plough . . . pack animals too weak to carry winter supplies to mountain villages. In advanced countries water-borne diseases have been almost banished and deserts made to bloom, but two-thirds of the world's population lack adequate and safe water supplies. As usual the greatest needs are in Asia, Africa and Latin America. A study in 75 developing countries showed that only 30 per cent of urban populations and less than 10 per cent of total populations had a piped water supply. Often it was only available for a few hours daily. These conditions are worsening as world poulation increases. In the 75 countries population is expanding almost 40 per cent faster than in the world as a whole. In the developing countries 500 million suffer yearly from water-borne diseases. They account for 5 million infant deaths a year. However, the World Health Organisation is confident that solutions can be found. Sufficient water resources are available in the world to make it possible to bring piped water to most people. Water technology is sufficiently advanced to make it unnecessary to wait indefinitely on further scientific research. "Capital, large as it is, can be raised. Personnel is available or can be rapidly developed. The major component now lacking is the will to translate these potentials into reality. Not lip service but militant action is needed."

There are some processes that man is not yet powerless to halt. We can still replant trees. Yet the trees of the world have been gradually disappearing as the centuries flow by. Suddenly the pace of destruction has quickened and the seemingly limit-less forests of North America and Brazil are being consumed at an alarming rate. We are living heavily on our capital of trees. The U.S. uses twice as much timber as she grows—a single issue of the *New York Times* [1] eats up 150 acres of trees. It seems very probable that in 50 to 60 years Europe's forests will be exhausted and in 80 to 100 years America's will be finished. As a result of cutting down trees, the area of desert in the world is now greater than the area of its forests. Today's paper will mean tomorrow's dearth : too much reading matter is a serious problem.

There is no danger of a shortage of capital, if we choose to use it aright. On both sides of the Atlantic personal savings are going up and up. We spend more on advertising than on educa-tion, more on coach trips than on building hospitals, more on tobacco than on the National Health Service. The economically advanced nations are setting aside about 10 per cent of their annual incomes in savings. Even allowing for a population in-crease at home of 2 per cent p.a. they only require about 5 per cent to maintain their domestic standards. They have, therefore, 5 per cent to spare for developing countries. It is probably true to say that the industrial development of non-white countries has

[1] A recent issue had 946 pages and weighed 7lb. 14oz.

scarcely begun as yet. The problem does not seem to be whether they can increase their production, but whether they can do it without adopting totalitarian forms of government. Of course efficiency is certainly an added problem. Java, for example, has greater natural advantages than Japan, yet has a rice yield per acre only one-third of Japan; and India is producing at only about 10 per cent of her capacity.

Within a comparatively few years the population problem will dwarf our present anxieties, even about nuclear weapons and Communist aggression. If present population trends continue, it seems likely that famine will reach serious proportions in India, Pakistan and China in the early 1970s, followed by Indonesia, Iran, Turkey, Egypt and several other countries within a few years, and then followed by most of the other countries of Asia, Africa and Latin America by 1980. Such a famine will be of massive proportions, affecting hundreds of millions of people. If this happens, as appears very probable, it will be the most colossal catastrophe of modern civilisation.

The world faces a food crisis before the end of this century. If steps are not taken to increase food production at a rate never before achieved, there could be world-wide famine in 20 or 30 years' time. There is no doubt that the world could grow enough food to meet all its needs; but doubts arise because the necessary effort to reach the targets may not be made. Effort depends largely upon health and capital. Man's war on disease is being hampered by lack of money. Here again is a *theological* problem. Better health means better cultivation: it also means longer life and more people: it may mean more famine in our lifetime. What is the good of doctors in India, for example, where 43 per cent of the population are under 15, reducing infant mortality if it only means that the children are more certain to starve as they grow up? Where is Christian responsibility? Japan has *halved* its birthrate by legalising abortion. Is this a Christian solution?

Certainly it seems that responsible family planning must be encouraged and developed—another instance of a world problem which obviously is both economic and theological. In all newly dependent countries of Africa and the Arab world, for example, the birth rate has remained unchanged since the start of the century, but the general death rate has fallen heavily and infantile mortality even more startlingly during the same period. The populations of these states are, therefore, increasing at a rate which means that they are bound to double every quarter of a century or so. The average number of children in a Tunisian family, for instance, was shown in the latest census to be 5.6, and it is not uncommon to find a woman bearing as many as 18 children. Some nations have already committed themselves to a family planning campaign on a national scale—India, Pakistan, Tunisia, Taiwan and Korea. In desperation the Indian Government has been forced to offer payments to husbands who agree to submit themselves to an operation for sterilisation. India's population is fast approaching 500 million and could double again by 1990.

Better food is needed to produce better scholars and better scholars are required to produce better food. To be a good scholar generally requires good health and to have good health requires a good training. So then the supply of food and water, the eradication of disease, the training of adults and the schooling of children are all interdependent and must progress together. This is what the various branches of the United Nations—the World Health Organisations, the International Labour Office, the Food and Agriculture Organisation and several others—seek to ensure together with emergency relief and community development schemes both urban and rural. The cost of all this runs into millions of pounds which can be well spent annually without extravagance or luxury.

The world of the nineteen-sixties is the biggest challenge to the affluent society. What are we doing about our prosperity and their poverty? Why is it political "suicide" to put Overseas Aid on political posters or in election speeches? Why are the starving millions overseas not a feature in any political election? Who would vote for a candidate for the Government of the nation who stood for sharing our prosperity with Asia or Africa? Most Christians in America and Britain are immensely wealthy com-

pared with our fellow-men in Africa and Asia. How concerned
are we about their problems?

"Lord, when was it we saw you hungry or thirsty or a
stranger or naked or ill or in prison and did nothing for you?
And he will answer, I tell you this: anything you did not do
for one of these, however humble, you did not do for me."

Only 30 years ago professional economists thought that the
future for developing countries was very bright, that most of
them had possibilities of enormous growth, and that the Western
world would be in danger of stagnation. This picture has
changed. Many economists are now pessimistic about the pros-
pects for developing countries. There are several main reasons
for this anxiety: (1) developing countries frequently lack overseas markets and their own people are too poor to buy products;
(2) there is often a lack of investment, so there are few factories
because the countries are too poor to save; (3) many countries
are relatively unproductive in agriculture because the people are
too badly fed to work properly; (4) there is generally a lack of
native technology, and adapting Western techniques has proved
very complicated. It is not just a simple question of "showing
the natives". What happens when we have built them shops and
they still prefer bazaars, or when we send a few million shovels
to people who go barefoot?

Until very recently it was thought that money would solve
everything. Give the developing countries the capital to build
themselves into industrial nations. However, very little experience was necessary before realising the limitations of building
factories in the midst of Africa and Asia. They do not function
by magic and it is difficult to get maintenance engineers or spare
parts. It is obviously not easy to obtain educated and experienced foremen, often because educated natives want to be white
collar workers. There is also the market problem of who is going
to buy factory goods from Africa or Asia. The present trend is
wisely trying to invest in human resources by improving health,
by encouraging community development and by providing
appropriate education—it is useless to teach Africans Latin! But
these trends are bringing very serious problems in many of the

developing countries. Improved health has caused the population explosion. Improved education causes the "literate unemployed" in India and certain African states because educated natives will not do manual work. There seems to be truth in the allegation that much aid to developing nations is very inefficiently administered and distributed. Indeed there seems very little chance that many of these countries will achieve even 2 per cent rate of economic growth during the rest of this century. Certainly the hard fact is that in the last 10 years the poorer countries have been losing ground whilst the prosperous countries have been progressing further ahead. The rate of growth for the exports of the developing nations was 3.6 per cent, the rate of growth for their imports 4.6 per cent. Their share in world trade in 1950 was 30 per cent but in 1964 it was 18 per cent.

Western foreign economic aid, in the form of inter-Governmental grants or heavily subsidised loans from relatively rich to relatively poor countries, is at present at an annual rate of about £2000–£2500 million, including about £200 million from the United Kingdom. Since 1946 Britain has given over £325 million in grants for development and welfare schemes to Commonwealth countries, of which education and health schemes formed the largest projects. In 1964–65 we gave £38 million in free aid to dependent territories and the Colonial Office estimate for 1965–66 is £40 million.[1] This represents a public contribution of about 18s. a year from everyone in Britain. (We spend 45 times as much on defence—against what?) In addition large sums have been loaned to developing countries; India, for example, has been extended credits so far valued at £235 million. There is also a good deal of public charitable giving overseas via such agencies as Inter Church Aid and the "Feed the Minds" campaign. In 1964 the Oxford Committee for Famine Relief allocated £2.4 million to overseas aid projects. £200,000 of this represented emergency grants to victims of hurricanes, racial disturbances and the like. Last year 301 agencies in 80 countries had benefited by grants and supplies from Oxfam. In 1965 18 million tons of food were sent abroad

[1] In 1965–66 our defence expenditure was £2120 million—almost a quarter of a million pounds every hour.

under the U.S. "Food for Peace" programme. This went to 100 million people, including 70 million children; it is now in its second decade, also making a substantial contribution to the development of commerical markets for American farm products.

Communication between nations is not easy, especially with regard to financial aid. Motives and actions can be selfish, and even when the intention is good and helpful it can still be misunderstood or treated with reserve, suspicion or even hostility. Often there is deliberate misrepresentation of one nation in another and this frustrates international dialogue and interdependence. A typical but trivial instance of misrepresentation today pokes fun at our Beatle and Rolling Stone styles. The Russian press reported: *"In the British Isles there has been a sharp increase in the number of people whose incomes do not enable them to go to the hairdressers regularly"*.

It is worth noting that our balance of payments deficit is aggravated by gifts, loans and investments overseas. Sterling reserves, which are for the whole sterling area, have never been adequate, but the deficit is much worse because of aid given to developing countries. In the first quarter of 1965 investment abroad accounted for 37 per cent of the total deficit for that period. The surplus on our national current trading account is not sufficient to cover the outflow of long term loans and private investment abroad, in addition to heavy defence costs overseas. Nevertheless it cannot be assumed that Britain is a particularly generous giver to developing nations. We usually charge high rates of interest (7–8 per cent), require the money to be used exclusively to purchase British goods, and sometimes there are "political strings" attached. France is a much more generous giver. Last year she gave £370 million in grants and loans, 1.4 per cent of her national income, whereas for this country the comparable figures were £160 million and 0.62 per cent. It is no compliment to Britain that we should fall so far behind (see note on page 166).

Does financial aid really help developing countries? Of course it salves our Christian consciences that we should be giving them little handouts from our affluence to scratch the surface of their poverty. Of course it is politically expedient because Western

L

security is just as much at stake as Afro-Asian welfare. But has any amount of economic aid, on however generous a scale, had the slightest chance of galvanising Asia and Africa into a condition of self-sustaining growth? No amount of dollars or pounds can overcome the tragic implications of the *timing* of colonial withdrawal. "The Western Powers were persuaded, or persuaded themselves, to abdicate their mission and hand over control to local rulers (whose ambitions scarcely exceed the primitive goal of feathering their own nests) just at the moment when their physical resources and surplus wealth had become large enough to transform the under-developed world; they did so at the precise point in history when Western man had so harnessed nature that he enjoyed the technical know-how and power to revolutionise the lives of the backward peoples with a speed and on a scale almost comparable to the original act of divine creation." This is the verdict of one observer. It may well be the verdict of future historians. They may come to see foreign aid as a forlorn Western attempt to escape the consequences of the tragically lost opportunities of 1945–65. This is not written in a spirit of contempt or blame. The religious, cultural, social, historical, climacteric—not to mention economic and political—obstacles barring progress in Asia and Africa are of a dimension that is beyond many Westerners' capacity to grasp. It has been estimated, for example, that the Paris of 1789 had more skilled industrial labour and experienced management than that supplied by the 100,000,000 people of Indonesia today; and that Elizabethan England could boast a more scientifically orientated population than contemporary India.

But surely financial help from developing Western nations to other developing nations is better than nothing? This does not seem to be self-evident. Is there not a danger that encouragement of the West to believe in the relevance of foreign aid, even as a partial solution, when in truth it is no solution at all, engenders a false sense of complacency which in turn precludes any genuine attempt to find realistic answers? Is there not a danger, too, that Western involvement on a wholly unrealistic basis with the deepening tragedy of the developing countries will cause us to be blamed (and to blame ourselves) for developments wholly outside our control? And is there not the danger that Britain and America, increasingly discouraged by the mounting evidence of the futility of noble endeavour overseas, will allow the consequent frustrations and disappointments to infect our faith in our own destiny?

One country has prompted the questions of the two previous paragraphs. Which is the one non-Western coloured country that has successfully broken through into the modern world? Japan. How did it do it? By its own drive and energy, without foreign aid. Why did it do it? Because it could no longer tolerate being pushed about by the Western powers. But what would have happened to Japan if the West, instead of seeking to exploit its backwardness and weakness, had sweetly offered to help with foreign aid? Perhaps nothing would have more certainly slowed down Japan's pride-propelled ascent into the modern world. Is it not possible that Western charity to the under-developed world today, while quite insufficient to bring about self-sustaining growth, is just enough to satisfy national pride, particularly since so much of it goes into such status symbols like airlines and armies? In other words foreign aid may be dulling the one incentive that once worked an economic miracle in Japan, and might work elsewhere if only the West did not feel compelled to smother it with kindness.

International competition from Japan is probably only just beginning, even though Japanese exports have risen 15 per cent p.a. for the past decade. The whole pattern of the Japanese economy has been changed. The really dramatic increases in exports have been by the newer industries—machinery up 900 per cent—since 1956, chemicals up nearly 800 per cent, metallic goods over 600 per cent. Nevertheless the most resounding successes have been secured in the very products which have been expanded most in the domestic market, and by far the greatest effort by Japanese industry has gone into meeting the demands of home consumers who have been enjoying a period of un-exampled prosperity. Electric household appliances rarely existed until the 1950s in Japan. Now nine out of 10 urban households have a television set, seven out of 10 a washing-machine, and one in two a transistor radio. Tokyo, with nine television channels, most of them going full out from 6.30 in the morning, is reported to have more sets than households, and also the world's fastest trains.

Japan herself is facing serious problems. Her economy in 1966–67 is grappling with all the difficulties of affluence and rapid expansion. It remains to be seen whether she will adopt the "cut taxation" policy of America or the "credit squeeze" economics favoured by Britain.[1]

There are those who still feel that if only we would give enough assistance quickly enough, the problem of Asia and Africa would be solved and the growth of Communism and Islam would stop. Unfortunately such a world solution is not so simple. A real solution can come only through the development of new structures of political, social and economic life which will be capable of bringing order out of chaos and of establishing a more just society. Thus there seem to be special areas in which Christian faith has special relevance to the revolutionary situation of developing countries. Indeed Christianity has already begun to exercise a marked influence even in some lands in which the Christian minority is very small. Three such contributions are most obvious:

1. *Christianity is injecting the ideal of service into Public life*

The ideal of the "public servant" is so much a part of our Transatlantic tradition that we take it for granted. We do not realise how much we are indebted to Christianity for it, nor what chaos and corruption reigns in public life when it is not present. In quite a few of the developing countries there does not exist, in the language of the country, a word for "public servant". Rare indeed is the politician or doctor, teacher or agriculturalist, who conceives of his work as primarily an opportunity for service; rarer still is the man in public life who uses his position primarily to serve his country rather than himself. Consequently, corruption in government is often rampant and our finest programmes of assistance often accomplish so little. It would be a

[1] In 1966–67 Japan is spending 1.6 per cent of her annual income on defence, compared with the U.K. figure of 7.2% and U.S. 8.2%.

great mistake to infer from this that such dedicated public
servants do not exist in every country in the world. But the
fact that they are so few explains in part the seriousness of
the present situation, and is one of the reasons why Marxist
Communism often has such power and appeal. In many instances, it appears as the only political force capable of ending
corruption and developing a sense of service to a cause. But in
the lands of the younger Churches, Christianity is quietly doing
this job. Christians in public life are known as men of integrity
who cannot be easily bribed and who fight against corruption.

2. *Christianity creates a sense of responsibility in ordinary people*
     When a peasant in a developing country is converted to Jesus
Christ, something happens which overcomes his lethargy and
breaks the bonds that enslave his spirit. He decides to learn to
read in order to study his Bible, he thus begins to educate himself, and he decides to send his children to school. He is no longer
the victim of total despair in the face of his situation, and he
begins to concern himself about solving his problems. And in
the little community of believers to which he belongs, which
often depends almost entirely on the lay leadership, he partici-
pates in a school of democracy and responsible living that pre-
pares him to act intelligently in political life as well.

3. *Christians active in politics can point out and help to over-*
   come the dangers inherent in the political structures of our day
     It is now quite evident that there are certain dangers inherent
in the new political, social and economic structures which are
spreading across Africa and Asia. We see this most clearly in the
Marxist Communism. This movement, which set out to estabilsh
perfect justice in the world, has brought even greater injustice.
In this situation, it is the Christian who should be most aware
of these destructive forces and most active in trying to overcome
them. He cannot be content with the excessive materialism of
our time, for he knows that human life cannot be reduced to
mere material existence, and he is called to seek first the kingdom
of God. His encounter with God in Jesus Christ reveals to him
the true meaning of personal existence. The fact that God loves

us and concerns Himself about each one of us forces the Christian to work for a type of society in which such concern for the individual is possible. It also transforms him into a person who, participating in that society, injects this concern into all his activities.

Each one of us needs to be aware of the inevitable corruption of power in the modern state and the danger of making an idol of any political movement. We are personally related to and judged by a God who destroys all men's idols and shatters all human pretensions. We live daily by the experience of divine forgiveness, and our pride in our own welfare and achievements needs to be overcome by an awareness of divine mercy and grace. This experience provides Christians with a keen sense of the dangers in modern politics and makes it imperative that we work towards the establishment of a world in which excessive power and poverty will be checked. At the same time we proclaim to the nations the Lordship of One who demands that all human institutions be open to Him and do His will.

> *Go forth into the world in peace*
> *Be of good courage*
> *Hold fast that which is good*
> *Render to no man evil for evil*
> *Strengthen the fainthearted*
> *Support the weak*
> *Help the afflicted*
> *Honour all men*
> *Love and Serve the Lord*
> *Rejoicing in the power of the Holy Spirit.*

Note: During the period 1946–64 U.S. aid overseas amounted to $76,999 million. This included $47,186 million in grants and the remainder in loans payable over 40 years. These figures exclude $33,189 million in military aid overseas. In addition, economic aid to Viet-nam has cost the U.S. $2115 million in the past 10 years: the cost of military operations is classified information. During 1966–67 America is giving approximately $4000 million in overseas aid, plus the cost of military aid. These U.S. figures amount to 0.63% of her national income (only 0.01% higher than the U.K.)

PART THREE

CHRIST IN AFFLUENCE

BY BRIAN K. RICE

CHRIST IN AFFLUENCE

THE key to the affluent society is the New Testament. This is our conclusion. Too often the Church is talking to itself about itself. But nothing happens. The world is unmoved. Little attempt is made within the Church even to identify the many gods of Western culture, to say nothing of exposing their falseness. Nevertheless, in spite of our preoccupation with the immediate problems of local congregations there is the growing recognition of the fact that the Church cannot live by itself and that, whether Christians like it or not, we are deeply affected by what is going on in the world. Thus witness and worship become doubly difficult because we live in a changing society in a changing world. There seems to be no stable ground or point of reference. And all too often Christ is relegated to being the Lord of another specialisation, the Sunday congregation in a few of our personal habits, but unrelated to the rest of life in society —to politics, business, pleasure, community affairs. Generally a "successful" Church is judged to be so by the members it attracts, the number of its organisations and activities, the prestige and popularity it enjoys rather than by whether it is living out its obedience to its Lord and so becoming not a reflection of society but the source of a profound critique of it.

For Christians a realistic analysis of the "signs of the times" cannot be a cause for despair. It is on the contrary a call for repentance and a call to important work. For God was and is at work in Christ reconciling our world to Himself. Affluence is the good gift of the Creator God, who is Himself the first and greatest Technologist. And God calls men to become actively involved with Him in the world for its redemption. Twenty-five years ago this was put by William Temple in terms of "How should the Church interfere?" Today interference has given way to involvement. It is in this context that we must continue to rethink the mission of the Church to the world. We cannot do it as separate Churches, nor as separate denominations, nor as younger or older Churches. As members of the universal

Church we must face a revolutionary situation that is universal :
most of the problems we have been discussing are international
worries, very few affect only America and Britain.

We have tried to discuss objectively something of the nature
and intensity of the signs of the times. We cannot escape such
confrontation. Many of the old structures of life have been
abandoned or are collapsing; new ones have not yet been born.
People stand between hope and despair; they look for a better
day but somehow tomorrow never comes. The times are pregnant with almost unlimited possibilities for good and for evil.
Christians are called to play a decisive role in society at every
level. But what are we to do? Suggestions at this point are not
wanting; we are constantly being offered new answers. But as
we see more clearly what is happening around us, we are
haunted by the thought that perhaps our most important problem is not just to know what we must do, difficult as that may
be. More disturbing is the question : Is there any reason why we
should do what we know we must, especially if it involves great
sacrifice and commitment on our part. And if we are willing to
get involved in these vexing matters, what can we hope to
accomplish ?

Our concern here is to look at the problems of prosperity as
Christians. Affluence in the hands of fallen man is a double-
edged blessing and the source of much evil. What does this
mean? Sometimes we are given to understand that Christianity
simply urges us to take the nineteen-sixties more seriously and
do something about our world. If this is all the New Testament
has to offer us, if it simply places still heavier burdens upon our
already-tired shoulders without facing the more fundamental
questions raised by our encounter with affluence, it can hardly
stir us to action in such times as these.

Our contention here is that the New Testament is speaking
to Christians in Britain and America in a quite different way.
As a point of departure, it offers us a *radically different perspective* from which to understand what is going on around us,
and calls us to participate in the life of the community of destiny
in which all our endeavours take on new meaning. Christianity
does not start out by putting burdens upon us; it offers us new

possibilities of life. It is not *Law* but *Gospel*. It is not a request for us to do something about the affluent society, but a message of what God has done, which completely changes the world situation. When the New Testament speaks to us, it calls us to look at the nineteen-sixties through the eyes of faith, to see the problems of prosperity in the light of what God is doing, to enter into the community which He has established and find our vocation in the order He has set up. What has God done which changes the world situation and provides us with new perspective from which to understand our encounter with affluence? The Message of the Second Assembly of the World Council of Churches, meeting in Evanston in 1954, expressed it thus:

Here where we stand, Jesus Christ stood for us. He came to us, true God and true man, to seek and to save. Though we were enemies of God, Christ died for us. We crucified Him but God raised Him from the dead. He is risen. He has overcome the power of sin and death. A new life has begun. And in His risen and ascended power He has sent forth into the world a new community, bound together by His Spirit, sharing His divine life, and commissioned to make Him known throughout the world. He will come again as Judge and King to bring all things to their consummation. Then we shall see Him as He is and know as we are known. Together with the whole creation we wait for this with eager hope, knowing that God is faithful and that even now He holds all things in His hand.

> *Thy Kingdom Come*
> *Thy Will be done on earth*

When we think about our mission in a revolutionary world, our thinking is determined by God's activity. This provides the context in which we may analyse Transatlantic problems and try to understand our responsibility. God is concerned about people in their affluence, in their need and in their suffering; He is the God of judgment and mercy who continually destroys unjust structures and opens new possibilities. He is at work in the historic process, leading towards fulfilment. This is the

supreme relevance of the New Testament to the nineteen-sixties :
namely that, "When Jesus saw the crowds, he had compassion
for them, because they were harassed and helpless, like sheep
without a shepherd".

To the extent that Christian thinking is determined by the
New Testament, the Christian will see the problems of the world
in a different light and will understand national and social responsibilities in a different way from that of our contemporaries.
Christians are compelled to assume a critical attitude towards the
affluent society and to strive to lead the community to a more
just programme of action. This constitutes the prophetic role of
the Church and one which we must accept as a most serious
and urgent responsibility. Refusal to do this means destruction ;
response to it gives us the possibility of becoming bearers of
God's will in our time. Nothing can be quite so serious as the
choice between these two possibilities. This is a most difficult
task. It is not usually easy for Christians to choose the right path
in any sphere of life, be it politics, community affairs, moral
standards, status or hardship. We always tend to see the situation
in terms that are convenient to us and our actions are likely to
be expressions of self-interest. Therefore God's will for us may
be different from what we are doing or want to do. Society
seldom admits that God is judging it ; it seldom welcomes
prophets with open arms.

The Jews stoned the Prophets and killed some of the bearers
of divine judgment. They were also led into captivity. In the
time of Jesus, even the most serious religious leaders failed. They
were so bound to the past and so anxious to preserve it that they
were unable to see what God was doing in their midst ; they
could not, as Jesus reminded them, "discern the signs of the
times". They were most zealous and possessed deep moral concern ; yet in the end this only led them to kill the person God
sent to show them what was really going on. They too paid the
price of their blindness. Today we can hardly hope that the
prophet will fare any better. In our encounter with affluence it is
hard for Christians to see that God is judging the Church. It is
much easier for us to take refuge in the past and strive to preserve the old pattern of life. As we do so, we may be convinced

that this is the only way to save society; to the eyes of prophetic faith, it is the surest road to destruction. Thus Christians must speak and act with a tremendous sense of urgency, and we can expect to be misunderstood.

We have received no special illumination that will show us what society must do in any given moment. We do not even have a neat set of principles to apply to every problem. We have only the perspective which the New Testament provides, which shows us the direction in which God's activity is going and in which our own responsibility lies, and the guidance of the Holy Spirit as we strive, in the fellowship of the community of believers, to discover God's will. Only to the degree that Christians all across the land meet together to study the problems of prosperity, think through the meaning of God's activity for them, and prepare for action in society, can we feel that we have been faithful to our commitment. Christians must remind the nation that we are today involved in a social revolution and that all our thinking about responsibilities in the world must take cognisance of that fact. God is at work in this revolution. It is partly a manifestation of His judgment upon exploitation, injustice and imperialism; it is also an opportunity for the development of a more just, social and economic order. Only as we understand what this means will we be able to act wisely. Our Western position of comfort and abundance does not prepare us for this task. The peoples across the world who are caught in this social revolution and see the dimensions of it are becoming more and more convinced that we cannot understand their situation.

The God of the New Testament is the God of social problems, of politics, of economic affairs, of international relations. These problems are theological problems and are among the most important areas of Christian obedience in our time. If the Church hopes to fulfil its prophetic function, we shall have to expose all efforts to blind mankind to the reality of God's activity in the present world, and expose them with the same vigour and courage with which the Prophets of Israel denounced the false prophets who tried to do the same thing to the Jewish people of their time. Regardless of how difficult this may be for Christians, we must do it courageously and humbly, knowing that we are on the side of those forces which are at work in the world and will determine its future.

If the Christian Church is to reveal a pattern of life in line with the New Testament and relevant to the nineteen-sixties, it must give priority to the study of political and economic problems and to action in these fields. We might go so far as to say that no believer in Jesus Christ has really understood the nature of his faith until he comes to feel the urgency of action in these fields. Surely it is vital that Christians read, think, write, discuss and pray about the world of economics and politics, and make an impact in these matters. How else is Christ to get through to the affluent society? Most Christian thinking about the impact of Christianity on the social state of man and on economic conditions is *from the past*—from Shaftesbury and Maurice, Gore and Temple, Tawney and Bonhoeffer. Fortunately the World Council of Churches is beginning to give a lead. In August, 1965, some 50 experts from all over the world gathered in Geneva for an "ecumenical confrontation" on Christian responsibility in earning and spending and in social action. This may well initiate a new era in the Christian critique of economic problems. At present we suspect that Christian thought is not contributing to the contemporary state of the debate in political and economic affairs in which the rest of the community is taking part; we believe that Christians must have political and economic views and must learn to express them.

A good Christian must be a good citizen. In the affluent society citizenship means politics and economics. These are problems of power in any institution, in the local community and in society at large. It is the question of getting and maintaining power and using that power for certain ends. For Christians politics have assumed special importance for several reasons: (1) All over the world the structures of economic, social and political life are changing. The Welfare State is a political institution. The development of new structures of community life is, in no small degree, a political question. The nature and ability of communities to meet the problems of a new day will depend upon what groups in society have power and how they will use it. (2) Governments now seem to have power over all realms of life and influence in every area of society, to an extent never imagined in former times. Thus today all problems are, to a certain degree, political problems, and solutions for them cannot come without political action. Whether Christians like this or not, it is a fact. Unemployment and inflation, education and nuclear weapons, foreign aid and import surcharges, religious and academic freedom; all these are today, in some sense, political matters. (3) In a democratic society all citizens play a decisive role in politics. We elect our representatives; our attitude on important issues determines in part the decision of our government, and our refusal to accept our political responsibility provides minority pressure groups with the opportunity they desire in order to secure legislation of which we do not approve and which is contrary to the common welfare.

Christians cannot, therefore, remain indifferent to political questions. The God of the Bible is the God of politics, and faith in Him implies action in those centres of power in which the direction of human events is determined. Thus the New Testaments speaks of rulers as ordained by God and urges Christians to pray for them. But there is one difference between our situation and that of those to whom the biblical writers addressed themselves. They saw the importance of the political sphere, but as the common people had no influence over government, they could do nothing but pray for their rulers. In a democratic society, anyone who is concerned enough about the political order to pray for it must also be active in politics. Moreover, Christian concern for others must lead to political action. Today, concern for the starving cannot rest content with supporting the Oxford Committee for Famine Relief or Inter Church Aid. It must also lead to political action to remove the causes of hunger. The prophetic role of the Church cannot be exercised by speaking boldly about the weakness of the government of the nation. Any awareness of such errors must lead us to do everything in our power to influence public opinion and to strengthen politically those forces which are most aware of what must be done.

If we are concerned about the fact that two-thirds of the world's people are undernourished, we can send food parcels abroad and support private assistance programmes. All this has its place. But Christian compassion for the starving must lead us to see that we are called upon to act politically to support Government assistance programmes, to encourage trade with developing nations and to help them as they strive to establish a more stable economic order. If this job is to be done, the local Christian community must be politically responsible. It must help its members to see why God's activity in human affairs demands political action of us, and also to understand the direction which such action should take if it is to bear witness to the Gospel. It should offer the possibility of serious and continual study of the most urgent political issues in a revolutionary world and bring the insights of Christian faith to bear upon them. This may well mean writing to Members of Parliament, inviting local government officials to meet Church organisations, co-operating with the area Council of Churches to provide an opportunity for local M.P.s and candidates to speak, even preaching about Christian responsibilities in politics—we ourselves frequently preach on this subject on the Sunday before a national or local election. It may also mean contact with diocesan representatives, clergy and lay, in the national government of the Church (Convocation, Church Assembly, General Convention). We have found all these lines of approach to be helpful and worth pursuing. Invariably M.P.s will send a full and comprehensive reply by return of post and local officials welcome the interest shown in the government of the community. There is a great deal of political apathy these days and politicians of all parties are being vexed by this lack of public concern. Whether the Church is now taking a livelier interest in matters political is perhaps doubtful, but it may not be without significance that in the national elections for Church Assembly and Convocation in November 1964 the average poll was 75–80 per cent compared with an average poll of 8–12 per cent in elections for key posts in trade unions.

Politics and economics mean for Christians and the Church the same kind of involvement in the conditions of human welfare that Jesus in His own earthly life exemplified. Political structures and economic activity are the ultimate and crucial test of the relevance of the Gospel. It is true that Christian responsibility in these areas pose the utmost difficulty; it is also true that failure here renders communication meaningless everywhere else. Christians *must* join in the rough-and-tumble of economics and politics, even though we may find ourselves working with those who do not share our faith. The impression is widespread that the Church is strangely silent unless its own interests are at stake. The voice of the Church might be listened to with more seriousness if its concerns evidently embraced the needs of all mankind.

If politics "embraces human conduct in its total social dimension", then surely we are committed to involvement? Indeed we may recall that for centuries politics and economics were conceived to be branches of theology. They are as much a part of the total life of the Church as liturgy or preaching, which are ordinarily—and mistakenly—regarded as "Church activities" *par excellence*. The affluent society is not the immediate focus of attention in the sanctuary, but unless it is recognised as part of the life offered to God in the sanctuary, that life is damned. We can go further. Our Saviour is the Son of Man, who has identified Himself with all humanity in its suffering and sorrows, its joys and victories, and in the ordinary events of day to day life. Christ is not "outside" or "above" politics and economics.

If Christians are to play a significant part in the affairs of state, we must work in groups. Jesus worked through a group. Power is exercised by individuals in groups. Citizenship is exercised in community, in groups, and groups often start with one person. *The value of one!* One can influence others. Parish churches could do far more by way of discussion groups, study projects, community efforts, family nights in mid-week. *One* with initiative can start this. Of course one is not enough; Our Lord knew this. But one is a member of groups—congregation, union, rotary, parent-teacher association, political party, supporters' club, local council of churches, shareholders, women's institute or townswomen's guild. These wield power in the community. They influence society in many ways. *And one person on one committee brings Christ into the midst*. Local groups are often part of nation-wide organisations which have great influence. The remarkable growth of consumer associations illustrates the power of small determined groups. Manufacturers take

M

immediate notice of *Which* reports—and of individual letters addressed to the "Complaints Department" (on the envelope, of course!). When the local group makes its views known at regional and national conferences, it begins to make a positive contribution to the nation's welfare. It can begin to crusade for more youth facilities, for more government aid overseas, for money for mental research, for larger grants towards marriage guidance. One person in one group can start a crusade.

The Christian community is called to provide the nineteen-sixties with a clear witness regarding the importance, meaning and dangers of affluence. In order to do this we must have serious concern for the material well-being of others at the same time that we give living examples of the fact that man does not live by bread alone. It is somewhat perplexing to note the contrast between ideal and practice at this point in Marxist Communism and Christianity. For the Marxist there is no other reality aside from the economic one; man's struggle for bread determines all else. And yet the Communist revolutionary, as he gives his life to this cause, reveals a spirit of concern and sacrifice which contradicts his philosophy. When Communism is victorious, however, this materialism has fatal consequences. It results in an exclusive emphasis upon production, which overcomes the concern for justice at the same time that it leads to the destruction of the very spiritual and moral values that might save the system from total corruption.

Christians, on the other hand, see the importance of material things, yet we profess to believe that man does not live by bread alone. Therefore we should provide examples to the world of the way in which Christian faith sets men free from the obsession with material possessions. This is not always what happens. Interest in spiritual things may free Christians from concern for the material well-being of our neighbour. We can even find a subtle justification for such lack of concern by insisting that what really matters is man's spiritual health. At the same time folk who talk in such terms often reveal the most amazing interest in material advancement in life! As a result the Christian community all too often presents no witness at all to a world obsessed with striving for material possessions.

When Christianity is presented to under-privileged people, its message regarding material things at times seems to be: the Gospel so transforms men's lives that it betters their economic conditions. We note that Modern Tithing is sometimes presented in terms of ever-greater financial rewards. These things may indeed be true, but they are not the only thing which Christianity has to say about materialism. Thus the sons and grandsons of the first humble converts may end up giving so much attention to their material well-being that they have little time for the faith which gave them this possibility. And they forget that Christ, being rich, became poor for our sake, and identified himself with us in all our needs in such a way that we who would follow Christ must also accept this same pattern in relation to our neighbours. This frequent lack of clear witness by the Church to the meaning of the material side of life constitutes an ironic situation. It allows the Communist in many parts of the world to steal the show as the one who takes human need seriously and responds to it, and it incapacitates us to warn a world obsessed with affluence of the dangers which lie ahead along this path. What can Christians do at this point? Here too the answer can come only as small groups, unable to be at ease any longer, study the biblical doctrine of material things and strive to express it in practice.

The question of bread for me is a material question. The question of bread for my neighbour is a spiritual matter.

Our future as the Christian community is bound up inseparably with the future of the rest of the world caught in the social revolution. Those nations in which the consequent crisis is most acute urgently need economic help and must develop new structures of social and political life. Yet in the last analysis their fundamental need is a spiritual one and their hope of finding permanent solutions to their most urgent problems lies in the discovery of those moral and spiritual resources adequate for the task. If this is true, then the destiny of this world of poverty and prosperity depends above all else upon the faithfulness of the Christian Church as the obedient bearer of God's purposes for the nations. When this becomes apparent to us, the world mission of the Church can be seen in the true light and our responsibility for its support takes on new dimensions. This new fact of the World Church understood in the light of God's purposes for history is the most revolutionary thing which Western Christians can discover, and it can only lead to a total reorientation of the life, thought and activity of any local congregation that dares to take it seriously. The ultimate destiny of the world, and of every country in it, depends upon the faithfulness of Western Christians and the strength of the younger Churches and our willingness to be thrust out into the world and crucified for it, so that God may act through us.

To speak of faithfulness we turn back to the Bible where we began. The more we search the Scriptures the more we realise that perhaps God intends poverty and prosperity to remain with us till the last and that He wills us to grow in faith and discipleship as we grapple with the signs of the times. Most of the problems which vex us are not only Transatlantic but biblical. They are present in the Prophets, they are present in the New Testament. The status-seekers began in the Garden of Eden and all the problems of abundance and affluence are present in Genesis. We have spent the past few weeks meditating daily on the Book of Amos. If ever there was an affluent society with an abundance of problems and a divine message, it was *then*—and the message applies to us. Read Amos and see.

But our main inspiration has been the New Testament. Here for us is the key to the affluent society. It is the New Testament which lights our way among the status-seekers, the starving, the delinquent, the wealthy, the divorced, the mentally ill. Only in the light of the Gospel are we able to discern the signs of the sixties and seventies. If we are to minister to the victims of society, it can be done only in the light of Christ. And this means back to the New Testament. We have tried to bring together the scholar's study, the housing estate, the mental hospital, society around us because these are united in mission. The theology of mission is being proclaimed on all sides: but we usually overlook the complementary truth of the mission of theology. This mission tells of Our Lord's commands:

You are the salt of the earth.
You are the light of the world.

Too often we act as though Jesus is saying, "Let your light so shine before the Church". How easy it would be to radiate the Christ for an hour a week on Sundays in the happy fellowship of Parish Communion and coffee hour—and then back to worship the car, the washing-machine, the garden, the telly, the overtime, the electric cooker.

We have been compelled to look to the New Testament for help and strength. The Gospel has not failed us. In Christ we find the new perspective, the new priority: in Him the strength to wrestle with poverty and prosperity. If we are willing so to organise our time that we come to the New Testament day by day, we shall come to the *Christ of the Affluent Society.* He meets us verse by verse, speaking to the problems of prosperity and poverty. The New Testament is alive to the nineteen-sixties: it gives hidden resources to grapple with affluence, inner resources which we would scarcely believe exist, let alone mobilise.

Wherein do we find this help and strength in the New Testament? We speak as fools. But there is a comfort of the Scriptures to be found by patience. So we venture to conclude with some of the passages which give the key to the sixties. But we would stress that as we are each encountering the signs of the times on different frontiers so we must come individually and corporately to receive the power from on high. These few passages may not speak deeply and meaningfully to all men, but they have given new inspiration and perspective to us in our particular place as missionaries in the affluent society. As Paul says, we speak as fools.

1. *The Wise Men*

"Then, opening their treasures, they offered him gifts, gold and frankincense and myrrh." (Matt. 2:11)

Yes, God called the wise and wealthy to Bethlehem. And they must have been very prosperous in the midst of poverty. Think of their education, their servants, their status, their precious gifts. They gave gifts out of their treasure; we are not told that they handed over all their worldly goods, or even half like Zaccheus. Is it too much to imagine the commercialism of the first Epiphany, all Bethlehem trying to make a quick profit out of the rich tourists from the East now that the Christmas crowds could no longer be fleeced? Yes, thank God that He called—and calls—the affluent to Bethlehem to rejoice, to worship and to offer.

> Therefore Christian men be sure
> Wealth or rank possessing
> Ye who now will bless the poor
> Shall yourselves find blessing.

2. *The Magnificat and The Benedictus* (Luke 1 : 46–55, 67–79)

Often a different translation brings fresh light. There is much in these canticles to challenge and probe :

> He has scattered the proud
> He has put down the mighty
> He has filled the hungry
> He has sent the rich away.

Yes
> *we believe that thou shalt come to be our Judge*
> *we therefore pray thee, help thy servants*
> *whom thou hast redeemed with thy precious Blood.*

Or the Benedictus and John the Baptist. Try inserting our own condition in this prophecy of the Holy Spirit—that we should be saved from our affluence and from the hands of keeping up with the Joneses . . . that we, being delivered from the hand of our abundance, might serve Him without fear . . . what does John say for the self-made, the successful? . . . "No one can receive anything except what is given him from above" . . . what does the Baptist say for status-seekers? . . . "He must increase, but I must decrease".

3. *Simeon and Anna* (Luke 2 : 22–38)

Yes, the old, the very old. For them, too, God had a place, a purpose, a promise and a peace. There is great need today to respect the place of the elderly. They have their place by the Christ-Child, they are important to the Lord's Christ, they are in living contact with the Holy Spirit. What a message for us as we grow old and near death. What a challenge to the Christian community and to individual homes and disciples. Do we give the elderly the same priority and pride of place as did our Heavenly Father? How does the compassion of the local Christian community for the aged compare with the concern shown by the Welfare State?

4. *Almost a Teenager*

"Now his parents went to Jerusalem every year at the feast of the Passover. And when he was twelve years old, they went up according to the custom." (Luke 2 : 41–51) What a lot there is here about the inevitable problems of growing up! Jesus did not tell Mary and Joseph that He was staying behind. They encouraged His independence by going a day's journey without checking up on Him. When they did start to look, it took them three days to find Him. Imagine the worry for His parents. Did they feel guilty? "What have we done to deserve this?" And Jesus wonders what all the commotion is about. We have often thought of this incident—the only one recorded of Our Lord as an adolescent—when we hear of parents finding it difficult to cope with independent offspring. When we hear of today's teenagers going off for the weekend without telling their parents where they have gone, it is strange to recall that Jesus took off for three days without telling anyone. When would He have returned to Nazareth had His parents not found Him? And interesting that the Temple was apparently the *last* place they expected to find Him. Jerusalem was a comparatively small city and it would be fascinating to know what sort of places and company they checked during three whole days of searching. Has this fragment of Our Lord's youth come down to us to comfort modern parents and to underline the inevitability of worrying about independent offspring who almost invariably take care of themselves. Just as the point of the parable of the Prodigal Son is really the Forgiving Father, so likewise is the episode of the

Boy Jesus in Jerusalem a lesson for fond parents today who often find their children a worry. The Temple incident might well be called "educating parents".

5. *Temptation* (Matt. 4 : 1–11)

The inevitability of temptation : Jesus was led to it by the Spirit. He could not contract out of the world, the flesh and the devil. And how modern were His temptations—materialism, status, false idols. It is good frequently to examine our lives in the light of these three temptations. What place is given to material comfort, to status, to the false god? Where do they figure in our priorities? We can see Our Lord's areas of temptation : can we recognise our own weakest spots? There is great value in looking at the Temptation narrative and then listing our weak spots, then praying "Lead us not into this temptation". Frankly we have always wondered whether Jesus found sex a temptation. If He came to face representative temptations in our day, perhaps sex would be one of them. It would certainly be representative for the teens and the twenties—Jesus' age group. Surely all men are guilty on this score. True we do not all have sufficient opportunity or provocation to commit fornication and adultery. But Christ does not judge merely by outward perversion and immorality. "What I tell you is this : If a man looks on a woman with a lustful eye, he has already committed adultery with her in his heart." Can a man be normal, even human, and *never* look on a woman? Surely we are all without exception guilty of adultery in Our Lord's eyes.

6. *No equality in heaven* (The Sower, Mark 4 : 1–9; The Talents, Matt. 25 : 14–30; Dives and Lazarus, Luke 16 : 19–30; The Two Sons, Matt. 21 : 28–32; Two Debtors, Luke 7 : 40–43)

There is very little equality in the New Testament and no mention of democracy in the early Church. Our Lord seemed to appreciate that we are not equal. Life could not go on if we were all the same : we must have different skills, aptitudes and personalities. The idea that all men are equal is not to be found in the New Testament; but the idea that men are unequal does not contradict the doctrine of the brotherhood of man. The parables speak to us of different talents, different debts, different circumstances, different attitudes. And we think of angels and archangels, cherubim and seraphim, elders and living creatures. So there seems every probability of a heavenly hierarchy where some are more equal than others.

7. *No Faith* (Mark 4 : 35–41 ; Luke 12 : 27–31 ; Matt. 16 : 5–12)

Jesus often rebuked His disciples, even the closest of them. Sometimes it was their lack of faith, sometimes it was hardness of heart and sometimes it was status or reward. Usually we are only too conscious of our own weak faith and hard selfishness. It prevents us from getting too depressed if we look at those who were closest to Jesus. Often their discipleship was every bit as feeble as our own. Yet Jesus trusted and used them and they played an essential part in His work. His followers did not stop being human; all their failings remained and Jesus often criticised their ignorance, pride, selfishness, or lack of faith. Does not this give us strength and assurance as we reckon with our own inadequacy in Christ's service?

> *Come to me, all whose work is hard, whose load is heavy and I will give you relief. Bend your necks to my yoke and learn from me, for I am gentle and humble-hearted; and your souls will find relief. For my yoke is good to bear, my load is light.*

8. *Places in Heaven* (Luke 10 : 25–37)

What must I do to be saved? We can never get over or round Our Lord's answer to this vital question. What He did *not* say is equally important—not go to church, not fast and pray, not even go to Holy Communion every week; no mention of faith. None of these spiritual disciplines are listed as necessary to salvation. This seems incredible—but true. Instead Jesus answered with the story of the Good Samaritan and then said, go and do the same yourself. This is the divine command to get involved—if we want to be saved. How often we overlook this in our desire to become a holy huddle, a Church talking to itself about itself. Even in the Ordination Service priests are bidden "to forsake and set aside (as much as you may) all worldly cares and studies". We have often wondered where the compilers of the Ordinal got this "forsake the world" doctrine. Certainly not the New Testament! Fortunately the exhortation also calls priests "to be messengers, watchmen and stewards of the Lord; to teach, and to premonish, to feed and provide for the Lord's family; to seek for Christ's sheep that are dispersed abroad, and for his children who are in the midst of this naughty world, that they may be saved through Christ for ever". What must I do to be saved? Our Lord's answer was very clear. Go out into the midst of this naughty world and spread love and compassion. If we truly care about other people we shall come to salvation.

9. *Mental Sickness* (Mark 7 : 24–30; Luke 8 : 26–39; Matt. 17 : 14–18; and many others)

Jesus was very concerned about mental disease—about folk possessed with devils, unclean spirits, epilepsy, worry. He was equally concerned about the friends and relatives of those who were mentally sick and about the family anxieties. When He sent the Twelve on a mission the one power He gave them was authority over unclean spirits . . . and they drove out many devils. Yes, Our Lord was in the midst of mental illness. In these days of widespread mental illness, it is a true comfort to know that the sick in mind were a top priority for Jesus. The healing work in psychiatric hospitals is a continuation of the healing ministry of Jesus. It is difficult and delicate ministry, to be undertaken in faith and prayer, and the sphere of mental illness needs the support of congregational prayers more than ever these days. This work is very dear to Our Lord. He does not intend us to be cosy and complacent. "Do not think that I have come to bring peace on earth; I have not come to bring peace but a sword. For I have come to set a man against his father and a daughter against her mother, and a daughter-in-law against her mother-in-law; and a man's foes will be those of his own household." These uncomfortable words sound as though they might have been spoken about mental tensions, yet this was probably the last thing on the Master's mind. He *did* bring peace and unity by casting out devils. Yet we must reckon with the probability that this side of heaven Jesus never intended us to be peaceful and happily content. There is very little bliss in the affluent society. We can be sustained in our tensions and anxieties by realising that Jesus had far more on His mind and must have frequently been vexed and worried. That is why He has compassion on today's worriers.

10. *Today's rich*

What was Our Lord's attitude towards possessions? Poverty is held in high esteem in the Beatitudes and in various parables and numerous ethical sayings in the Gospels. Nevertheless it is important to understand that this is no *mystique* of non-possession. We can verify this in the parade of both good and bad rich men through the Gospels and of poor men in both character-categories, sympathetic figures such as Zaccheus, Nicodemus, Lazarus and Joseph of Arimathea, all men of wealth, as well as unsympathetic rich men such as the one who wanted Jesus to divine an inheritance (Luke 12 : 13) and the one who let a beggar lie neglected at his gate (Luke 16 : 19–31). The compassion of Jesus was aroused both by the hungry and by the rich. He saw that alike in poverty or in wealth the soul might starve. Jesus knew economic problems at first hand. He had earned His living as a carpenter and His disciples were working men. He did not condemn the wise use of wealth; He praises the centurion who built a synagogue (Luke 7 : 1–10), and commends the business ability of the Unjust Steward (Luke 16 : 1–8). Dives is condemned, not because he is rich, but because he neglected to do good with his wealth. The story of the rich young man (Mark 10 : 17–27) points at possessiveness, not possessions, which is precisely the message of the saying about treasure and the "heart" in Matt. 6 : 21. Today's rich do well to ponder what Jesus had to say about God and Mammon :

Sacrifice (Mark 12 : 41–44)	Profits (Matt. 25 : 14–30)
Debts (Matt. 18 : 23–35)	Capital gains (Luke 9 : 23–27)
Worry (Matt. 6 : 25–34)	Income Tax (Mark 12 : 14–17)
Which? (Luke 16 : 13)	Estimates (Luke 14 : 25–33)
Security (Matt. 16 : 24–27)	Affluence (Luke 12 : 13–21)
Hardship (Mark 10 : 23–31)	Salvation (Matt. 19 : 16–26)

11. *Like Christ*

If only we could tackle the problems of poverty and prosperity as Jesus would have done. What would Jesus do today? How can we have the modern mind of Christ? Of course our Christian commitment comes primarily from God, from His grace and goodness given to us freely and abundantly. But it is easy to become cosy and complacent. How do we share grace and goodness? As we seek to relate Christian faith to affluent living, we may find the necessary stimulus and self-examination in 1 Corinthians 13, the great hymn of love, probably based on Christ's own personality. Any modern translation of this chapter is worth careful meditation if we are to be signs of the times.

We can go forward to face affluence in Christ's name if we go back to the Gospels. There is no other way forward. The only light for our path is the Light of the World. There is so much in Holy Scripture which has direct bearing on the nineteen-sixties, and this can give us the divine assurance that God is at work in all the opportunities and tensions of today. The command to go into all the world is the command to follow where He has gone before.

May we finish with a simple personal testimony? We spend most Sunday mornings in a mental hospital, both writers having ministered there. There on Sundays the Holy Communion is celebrated and the mentally ill draw near with faith in considerable numbers, about 15 per cent of the total hospital population. Christ is offered to the worried, the lonely, the guilty, the adulterers, the potential suicides, the drug addicts, the lost, the V.D. sufferers, the orphans, and all victims of society. And in this wonderful and mysterious way Christ comes. We know these patients, their problems and their past and we know that into their midst comes Christ as Healer and Friend. This is so movingly true on Sunday mornings that we feel nearer to God among these of His children than at any other time of the week. Here Christ meets the nineteen-sixties face-to-face and reconciles us to Himself.

We have been forced to go back to the Gospel to find strength and insight without which no Christian can wrestle with the problems of poverty and prosperity. Our Lord speaks anew and we have been truly surprised to discover how much of the New Testament is speaking directly and positively to the problems which are vexing Christians on both sides of the Atlantic. Material abundance is not an unqualified blessing. What hard demands it makes! Who then can be saved? Our Lord's reply is clear: "All things are possible with God". We have learned that this is true. In the centuries which have passed what miracles have been wrought in God's name! Faith *has* moved mountains. In the name of Jesus Christ, the impossible has been accomplished again and again. We need only to look at a thousand million people in the world who claim allegiance to the Christian religion. If only the twelve Apostles could be present to see! The teaching, healing, preaching, witnessing ministry goes on, generation after generation, to illumine minds, heal bodies, satisfy souls and to win the world.

Let us conclude with some sentences from the Laws of Life which Our Saviour Christ declares unto us, to which, as an acknowledgment that His Word is our Law whereof we are daily transgressors, we answer after each sentence, "Lord have mercy upon us".

The Lord your God is the only Lord; love the Lord your God with all your heart, with all your soul, with all your mind and with all your strength. This is the first and great commandment.

Lord have mercy upon us

The second is this: Love your neighbour as yourself.

Lord have mercy upon us

Unless you change your whole outlook and become like little children you will never enter the Kingdom of Heaven.

Lord have mercy upon us

The man who will not take up his cross and follow in My footsteps cannot be My disciple.

Lord have mercy upon us

If you will not forgive other people, neither will your Heavenly Father forgive you your failures.

Lord have mercy upon us

Beware! Be on your guard against greed of every kind, for even when a man has more than enough, his wealth does not give him life.

Lord have mercy upon us

Love your enemies, do good to those who hate you, bless those who curse you, and pray for those who treat you badly.

Lord have mercy upon us

This is my commandment: Love one another, as I have loved you.

Lord have mercy upon us

You must go on growing in Me and I will grow in you. For just as the branch cannot bear any fruit unless it shares the life of the vine, so you can produce nothing unless you go on growing in Me.

Lord have mercy upon us

Thus the affluent society can be redeemed by faith—and by our willingness to risk all for the Gospel. Christ has redeemed man, so that in his hands affluence may be used sacramentally as a means of expressing Christian love, both to God and man. But unless we use our abundant prosperity to magnify the Lord, we who are rich shall be sent empty away. This is our verdict on Christian Responsibility in an Affluent Society.

INDEX

DATE DUE